NEW PERSPECTIVES

Portfolio Projects for Soft Skills

NEW PERSPECTIVES

Portfolio Projects for Soft Skills

Beverly Amer

COURSE TECHNOLOGY
CENGAGE Learning™

Australia • Brazil • Japan • Korea • Mexico • Singapore • Spain • United Kingdom • United States

COURSE TECHNOLOGY
CENGAGE Learning™

Portfolio Projects for Soft Skills

Vice President, Publisher: Nicole Jones Pinard

Executive Editor: Marie L. Lee

Associate Acquisitions Editor: Amanda Lyons

Senior Product Manager: Kathy Finnegan

Product Manager: Leigh Hefferon

Associate Product Manager: Julia Leroux-Lindsey

Editorial Assistant: Jacqueline Lacaire

Director of Marketing: Elisa Roberts

Senior Marketing Manager: Ryan DeGrote

Developmental Editor: Fran Marino

Senior Content Project Manager:
    Jennifer Goguen McGrail

Composition: GEX Publishing Services

Art Director: Marissa Falco

Text Designer: Althea Chen

Cover Designer: Marissa Falco

Copyeditor: Suzanne Huizenga

Proofreader: Kathy Orrino

For product information and technology assistance, contact us at
Cengage Learning Customer & Sales Support, 1-800-354-9706
For permission to use material from this text or product, submit all requests online at **www.cengage.com/permissions**
Further permissions questions can be emailed to
permissionrequest@cengage.com

Some of the product names and company names used in this book have been used for identification purposes only and may be trademarks or registered trademarks of their respective manufacturers and sellers.

Microsoft and the Office logo are either registered trademarks or trademarks of Microsoft Corporation in the United States and/or other countries. Course Technology, Cengage Learning is an independent entity from the Microsoft Corporation, and not affiliated with Microsoft in any manner.

Disclaimer: Any fictional data related to persons or companies or URLs used throughout this book is intended for instructional purposes only. At the time this book was printed, any such data was fictional and not belonging to any real persons or companies.

Library of Congress Control Number: 2011925424

ISBN-13: 978-1-111-58155-8

ISBN-10: 1-111-58155-X

Course Technology
20 Channel Center Street
Boston, MA 02210
USA

Cengage Learning is a leading provider of customized learning solutions with office locations around the globe, including Singapore, the United Kingdom, Australia, Mexico, Brazil, and Japan. Locate your local office at:
international.cengage.com/global

Cengage Learning products are represented in Canada by Nelson Education, Ltd.

To learn more about Course Technology, visit **www.cengage.com/course technology**

To learn more about Cengage Learning, visit **www.cengage.com**

Purchase any of our products at your local college store or at our preferred online store **www.cengagebrain.com**

Printed in the United States of America
1 2 3 4 5 6 7 8 9 15 14 13 12 11

Preface

The New Perspectives Series' critical-thinking, problem-solving approach is the ideal way to prepare students to transcend point-and-click skills and take advantage of all that application and soft skills have to offer.

The goal of this new Portfolio Projects text is to provide review of critical soft skills concepts, hands-on instruction using selected applications to teach skills related to the concepts, and multiple exercises to give students many opportunities to put the concepts and skills they've learned into action.

With the New Perspectives Series, students understand *why* they are learning *what* they are learning, and are fully prepared to apply their skills to real-life situations.

About This Book

This book provides a thorough, hands-on overview of soft skills concepts and applications, and includes the following:

- Five projects designed to teach students how to develop essential soft skills, including written and oral communication, critical thinking, and presentation skills
- A DVD with six unique videos and data files for the related exercises at the end of each project
- Real-world exercises reinforce student learning by using Office 2010 applications to practice customer service skills, negotiation skills, conflict management techniques, problem-solving steps, and decision-making processes
- A summary exercise called "My Portfolio" in which students create a personal portfolio of their best soft skills assignments to showcase their work to prospective employers

System Requirements

This book assumes a typical installation of Microsoft Office 2010 and a typical installation of Microsoft Windows 7 Ultimate using an Aero theme. (Note that most tasks in this text can also be completed using the Windows 7 Home Premium or Professional editions.) The browser used for any steps that require a browser is Internet Explorer 8.

www.cengage.com/ct/newperspectives

The New Perspectives Portfolio Projects Approach

Context
Each project focuses on a specific soft skill, such as preparing for an interview, organizing a presentation, or developing a business document, and provides students with seven distinct exercises.

Document Essentials
Each project includes extensive conceptual information that provides students with practical tips and techniques for creating the project document. Numerous figures provide examples for students to adapt. Tables present document creation guidelines in an easy-to-read format that students can immediately apply.

Key Points
Key Points, which appear in the margin in labeled boxes, offer expert advice and best practices to help students better understand how to create useful business documents.

Technology Skills
Each project includes a Technology Skills section, which provides hands-on coverage of a set of software skills related to the project document. Examples of technology skills include how to use online application tools, how to create and maintain an online persona, and how to track changes in Microsoft® Word.

Tips
Tips, which appear in the margin in labeled boxes, provide helpful hints and shortcuts for more efficient use of the software. The Tips appear in the margin at key points throughout the Technology Skills sections to provide students with extra information when and where they need it.

Assessment
Each project includes seven exercises: a Technology Skills exercise, a Practice exercise, a Revise exercise, a Create exercise, and three case studies.

My Portfolio
The text concludes with a summary exercise, My Portfolio, in which students select documents they have completed in the projects or create new documents to include in a personal portfolio. Students can then use their portfolios to demonstrate to current or prospective employers their soft skills and related software skills, showcasing their capabilities and talents.

Our Complete System of Instruction

CourseCasts – Learning on the Go. Always available...always relevant.
Want to keep up with the latest technology trends relevant to you? Visit our site to find a library of podcasts, CourseCasts, featuring a "CourseCast of the Week," and download them to your mp3 player at http://coursecasts.course.com.

Our fast-paced world is driven by technology. You know because you're an active participant—always on the go, always keeping up with technological trends, and always learning new ways to embrace technology to power your life.

Ken Baldauf, host of CourseCasts, is a faculty member of the Florida State University Computer Science Department where he is responsible for teaching technology classes to thousands of FSU students each year. Ken is an expert in the latest technology trends; he gathers and sorts through the most pertinent news and information for CourseCasts so your students can spend their time enjoying technology, rather than trying to figure it out. Open or close your lecture with a discussion based on the latest CourseCast.

Visit us at http://coursecasts.course.com to learn on the go!

Instructor Resources
We offer more than just a book. We have all the tools you need to enhance your lectures, check students' work, and generate exams in a new, easier-to-use and completely revised package. This book's Instructor's Manual, ExamView testbank, PowerPoint presentations, data files, solution files, figure files, and a sample syllabus are all available on a single CD-ROM or for downloading at http://www.cengage.com/coursetechnology.

SAM: Skills Assessment Manager

SAM is designed to help bring students from the classroom to the real world. It allows students to train and test on important computer skills in an active, hands-on environment.

SAM's easy-to-use system includes powerful interactive exams, training, and projects on the most commonly used Microsoft Office applications. SAM simulates the Office application environment, allowing students to demonstrate their knowledge and think through the skills by performing real-world tasks, such as bolding text or setting up slide transitions. Add in live-in-the-application projects, and students are on their way to truly learning and applying skills to business-centric documents.

Designed to be used with the New Perspectives Series, SAM includes handy page references, so students can print helpful study guides that match the New Perspectives textbooks used in class. For instructors, SAM also includes robust scheduling and reporting features.

Acknowledgments

Development of *Portfolio Projects for Soft Skills* required a dedicated and talented team of professionals (all of whom have wonderful "soft skills!") to revise this book's predecessor, *Soft Skills at Work: Technology for Career Success* into the resource you now hold in your hands. In particular, Marie Lee and Leigh Hefferon from Cengage Learning provided the vision and guidance to fit soft skills concepts into the *Portfolio Projects* model. Fran Marino once again provided developmental expertise and kept the project on track.

At Northern Arizona University, my faculty colleagues provided both ideas and insights to improve the pedagogy and class-test the content of the workbook and its projects. The video productions teams at Edit Alchemy and Aspenleaf Productions worked tirelessly to turn the Encore case study into a *Telly* award-winning video series recognized for both educational and production excellence.

Finally, my sincere thanks go out to instructors who recognize the importance of helping students develop their soft skills before entering the job market and work tirelessly to infuse their curricula with these projects because they know it's the right thing to do and are willing to do what it takes to make a difference in the lives of their students. You are my inspiration!
– Beverly Amer

TABLE OF CONTENTS

Why Soft Skills Matter: Career Preparation

Introduction

Most people enter college with the goal of graduating and securing their dream job. If you are reading this book, chances are good that you're one of these people. You're taking classes and learning methods, models, tools, and techniques that you can apply to real work situations down the road. These classes and their activities represent an investment in your future—one you're willing to make because you see the future payoff.

Yet there's more to landing that dream job than simply completing your coursework and earning good grades: You'll need to interview for prospective jobs—and to do that, you must learn how best to prepare and present yourself. This requires combining the technical skills you're gaining in school with "soft skills." But, what exactly are soft skills? **Soft skills** are the skills, abilities, and traits that relate to behavior, attitude, and personality. College recruiters and industry experts agree that solid written and oral communication skills top the list, followed by team skills, problem-solving and critical thinking skills, and work ethic. As you'll discover as you complete this workbook and start your career, you won't stand a chance of succeeding in your chosen profession without them.

In the next section, you'll get acquainted with a company called Encore Consulting. It recruits new college graduates just like you for consulting positions across a variety of industries. At the end of this project, watch the two short videos of a typical day in the life of an on-campus recruiter at the company, and critique the preparation and performance of the students being interviewed for consulting positions by using the information in the project. You'll decide what they did right—and wrong—and what behaviors are worth copying.

STARTING DATA FILES

Project.01

Resume_Template_01.docx
Practice_01.docx
Practice_02.docx
Revise_01.docx
VideoCritique_Worksheet_01.docx

Encore Consulting: Video Episodes 1a and 1b

Encore is a professional services firm, which means it provides consulting services to other businesses. The firm's services range from providing information systems solutions to providing strategic business planning and management consulting. Encore typically hires a small number of college students right after graduation to work as consultants on teams. Corporate recruiter Candace Johnson is on campus to interview several students for positions with the firm. In video episode 1a, three students—Matthew, Jill, and Sophie—are waiting to meet with Candace. Video episode 1b features a fourth student—Tony—at a different campus, in the process of being interviewed by Gerry West, another Encore recruiter.

Before you watch the video episodes, though, work through this project chapter and fill in the boxes with your own personal thoughts, opinions and reflections. When you watch, use the Video Critique Worksheet at the end of this project to analyze the preparation and performances of Matthew, Jill, Sophie, and Tony—the students who are interviewing for consulting positions with Encore. If needed, use the start file provided (VideoCritique_Worksheet_01.docx) with the Project.01 Data Files. Finally, use your analysis and this project's pointers to determine how you would prepare if you were interviewing with the company.

What a Résumé Does for You

KEY POINT

The goal of a résumé is to get an interview.

Depending on the career path you've chosen, there may be great demand for workers with your skills; however, that demand does not automatically translate into an easy start on that path. It's safe to assume there will be others applying for the position you're seeking. In fact, for some careers there are more than 70 applicants for every job opening! Most job openings for professional positions require applicants to supply a current résumé that provides company recruiters with an initial picture of who you are, what experiences and education you've had, your accomplishments, and the skills you bring to the company. What you write on your résumé determines whether you get a shot at an interview or your résumé ends up in the circular file (aka the trash).

Your résumé is a written document that clearly presents your qualifications for a position along with your ability to use those qualifications for the benefit of the company. Its purpose is to compel the company's recruiter to meet you to determine how well you'll fit in and whether you'll add value to the enterprise. In a sense, it's your own personal sales brochure that tells potential employers why they need you on their team. As long as your résumé is well written and you're qualified, you should get a shot at an interview.

What career are you hoping to pursue after college? What are some of the main qualifications and characteristics of people who have this career? How do you compare?

_____

_____

_____

_____

What a Good Résumé Contains

Most company recruiters spend less than 30 seconds scanning the résumés they get. This means your résumé must be organized, clear, and concise so the recruiter can easily size you up. You can format your résumé one of two ways: chronologically or functionally. A **chronological résumé** organizes your qualifications by date. Jill Tanner, from the Encore video, prepared hers using this format (Figure 1-1). This makes it simple for the reader to follow your history—whether that history comprises time spent in school or working. This format is particularly useful when you have acquired experience over time in a series of positions and is the most common format used by job seekers, particularly those who are right out of college.

| Figure 1-1 | Example of a chronological résumé |

Jill Tanner
15066 McConnell Circle
Reno, Nevada 89509
(775) 555-1445
jtanner@ureno.edu

Objective
Entry-level investment analyst position in a regional or national financial investment company.

Qualifications
- Financial analysis skills
- Ability to translate financial language into terms clients understand
- Team leadership experience
- Ability to develop detailed plans and meet deadlines
- Detail-oriented work ethic
- Creative and skilled writer

Work Experience
e-Vestments, real estate investment company, *customer service representative*, May 2011 – present
- Developed schedule for regular review of small (less than $100,000) client portfolios
- Created standard PowerPoint presentation on investing basics for employees speaking at local service club luncheons, such as Rotary and Kiwanis
- Researched investment options for clients
- Analyzed investment portfolio performance for clients with net worth up to $1 million
- Wrote company's quarterly investor newsletter to generate interest in company's real estate investment services

Small Business Administration, *volunteer business analyst*, October 2009 – August 2010
- Prepared financial statements and business plans for clients seeking SBA loans
- Coordinated teams of volunteer business analysts while working part-time at the Small Business Administration

Education
University of Reno, Reno, Nevada
    B.S., Business (Finance), December 2012
    Overall GPA: 3.52/4.00
    Courses include: Investing for Individuals, Real Estate Finance and Investment, Financial Analysis and Working Capital Management, Corporate Financial Management, Financial Statement Analysis

Extra-Curricular Activities, Certifications, and Awards
- Team Captain, University of Reno women's golf team, August 2011 – present
- Microsoft Office Specialist certification, Excel 2010, November 2010
- Women's Athlete of the Year, Sierra region, May 2011

References
Available upon request

In a **functional résumé**, your qualifications are structured into categories of skills that the employer might find desirable for the open position. Jill also formatted her résumé this way to highlight her skills (Figure 1-2).

Figure 1-2	Example of a functional résumé

Jill Tanner
15066 McConnell Circle
Reno, Nevada 89509
(775) 555-1445
jtanner@ureno.edu

OBJECTIVE
To obtain an entry-level investment analyst position in a regional or national financial investment company.

EXPERIENCE
• Researched investment options, including exchange-traded funds, for student team projects and clients
• Analyzed investment portfolio performance for clients with net worth up to $1 million
• Wrote company's quarterly investor newsletter to generate interest in company's financial services

ORGANIZATIONAL
• Maintained detailed spreadsheets linked to the Web with stock portfolio investment performance data
• Coordinated teams of volunteer business analysts while working part-time at the Small Business Administration

PLANNING
• Developed schedule for regular review of small (less than $100,000) client investment portfolios
• Created standard PowerPoint presentation on investing basics for employees speaking at local service club luncheons, such as Rotary and Kiwanis
• Prepared financial statements and business plans for clients seeking SBA loans

EMPLOYMENT
May 2011 – present, e-Vestments, real estate investment firm, *customer service representative*
October 2009 – August 2010, Small Business Administration, *volunteer business analyst*

SKILLS
Strong customer service orientation
Detail-oriented
Inquisitive and analytical acumen
Advanced Excel 2010 skills (Microsoft Office Specialist certification, November 2010)

EDUCATION
University of Nevada, Reno, Reno, Nevada
    B.S., Business (Finance), December 2012
    Overall GPA: 3.52/4.00

Regardless of which format you choose, a good résumé will contain the following items:

Heading

Your name, address, telephone numbers, and e-mail address should all be included to make it easy for the company's recruiter to reach you. If you have a school address and a home address, it is fine to include both of them.

Most often, the heading is centered at the top of the page in a bold and larger font than the body of the résumé. If your school permits the use of your academic e-mail address for job correspondence, use it. Don't include a photograph of yourself unless your appearance is a bona fide job requirement, such as in modeling or acting careers. Otherwise, the company may have to reject you in order to comply with hiring anti-discrimination policies and laws. Also avoid inappropriate and unprofessional e-mail addresses that are quirky or juvenile, such as "partyboy7" or "babyshuga." Why? Think about what such addresses say to a potential employer about your personality, maturity, and professionalism. Instead, go with a low-risk Gmail or other account for your job search using your first and last name.

What type of résumé format do you think would work best for you? Write down what your heading will contain.

_____

_____

_____

_____

Objective

Usually no more than one or two sentences, your objective gives potential employers an idea of the type of job you are seeking. Consider the following objective statement for someone applying for an entry-level systems analyst position:

Objective: To obtain a position as an entry-level systems analyst in an international management consulting company.

This objective plainly tells the reader what type of company the applicant wants to work for, the job level, and the position this person is seeking.

Avoid using phrases such as "growth opportunity" or "challenging position" as these are generally regarded as too vague to be meaningful. You can make your objective even more compelling by personalizing it for a specific company. For example:

Objective: To obtain a position as a systems analyst at Encore Consulting, Inc.

Write your objective statement here.

_____

_____

_____

_____

Qualifications

This section briefly describes your experience and the kinds of skills you offer the company. A bulleted list is most effective in organizing your qualifications for easy reading. There is no need to be verbose here. You'll have the opportunity to explain your experience and skills in greater detail in the next section. Jill's résumé in Figure 1-1 gives examples of some bulleted qualifications she prepared based on her background and experiences.

> Conduct an online search for career qualifications. Which ones best describe you?
>
> _____
>
> _____
>
> _____
>
> _____

Section Headings

Whether you use the chronological or functional résumé format, section headings will provide a logical structure to the body of your résumé. In a chronological résumé, the section headings might consist of Education, Work Experience, Organizations, or Volunteer and Community Service. In your Education section, be sure to spell your school names correctly and fully, with city and state information. Most recruiters like to see a grade point average (GPA) included, whether it's your overall GPA or the GPA in your major courses. Indicate the scale used, such as a 3.42/4.00 scale. Most often, anything below 3.00/4.00 isn't worth mentioning—but to be sure, ask your professor or a Career Services counselor, or do an online search to see what is recommended. The cut-off point varies by company and industry. If you have relevant work experience, like Jill does in Figure 1-1, list it at the top of your résumé. Otherwise, put your education first.

In a functional résumé, the section headings might be Systems Analysis, Programming, Consulting, Project Management, or other descriptive titles. The skills and experience you list in these functional areas should be broad enough so that the recruiter can easily see how they would be relevant for the open position as well as the future needs of the organization.

> Which résumé format is best for your background and experience level? List the section headings that best fit your background and experience.
>
> _____
>
> _____
>
> _____
>
> _____

Descriptions

This is where the employer will see your accomplishments and successes. You want to convey that if you were able to achieve great things in the past, you also will do so in the future. The keywords you choose can help demonstrate your ability. Underneath each heading, describe your experience and skills using action verbs. For example, words such as "managed," "organized," "planned," and "wrote" are strong and active. Figure 1-3 lists common action verbs for résumés, but longer lists can be found by searching online. If you supervised employees or managed financial resources, say so. If you identified a problem and came up with the solution, describe it. Emphasize what you accomplished and why this was of value to your employer.

Avoid phrases such as "Duties included" or "Responsibilities were" as they are weak and ineffective in conveying the nature of your experience. For example, if you worked at the drive-thru window of a fast-food restaurant, you might say, "Managed the accuracy and delivery of drive-thru orders for (name of restaurant) with a team of three employees. Consistently met customer service order delivery targets of 90 seconds or less and handled 65% of total lunchtime business for the restaurant." This is preferable to stating that your responsibilities included order taking, cash handling, and food delivery.

Figure 1-3	Common action verbs for résumés		
Analyzed	Assisted	Built	Collaborated
Coordinated	Created	Coordinated	Designed
Developed	Examined	Formulated	Generated
Handled	Implemented	Kept	Launched
Maintained	Negotiated	Organized	Performed
Planned	Raised	Researched	Repaired
Scheduled	Streamlined	Studied	Supervised
Taught	Updated	Verified	Wrote

Look at Figure 1-3. Which of these action verbs describe what you have done? What others can you find online?

_____

_____

_____

_____

Other Skills and Qualifications

This last section provides a place to list items that don't neatly fit into other categories. For example, your ability to speak Spanish fluently goes here, along with your membership in professional organizations, publications you've contributed to, your community service activities, and honors or certifications you've earned. It's fine to include accomplishments that are not directly job-related that could help you stand out, such as being a finalist on a reality TV show, qualifying for the Olympics, or organizing a charity fundraising event for the local animal shelter. They often pique the interest of the interviewer and can help break the ice at the start of your meeting.

References

You must provide the names and contact information for several individuals who can attest to your personal and professional qualifications, if asked. However, they should not be listed on your résumé; it's sufficient to state "References available upon request." But those references should be printed out and ready to deliver when this request is made, whether at the interview or later. Be sure to approach your potential references ahead of time to get their permission and give them a copy of your résumé. Let them know when you are called for an interview so they are not caught off-guard when the company calls to get their input on your qualifications.

List the names, addresses, and phone numbers of at least three people who could serve as references for you.

_____

_____

_____

_____

What if you've never worked or you don't have many qualifications? Now is the time to remedy this situation. Volunteer, seek an officer position in a school club, or take on a part-time job to get some work experience. Employers who compare the résumés of two students—one who is a straight-A student without any other experiences, and one with a lower GPA but who worked during school or served in a variety of extra-curricular positions—will usually choose the more well-rounded student. Why? Having multiple responsibilities proves that you are capable of juggling many different priorities, which underscores your ability to manage your time well. Life after college is all about time management and priorities, so working on these skills now makes you better equipped to handle the demands of work and life once you graduate.

> **KEY POINT**
>
> Having mistakes or errors on your résumé guarantees you won't get an interview.

The most common mistakes people make on résumés range from grammatical errors to outright fabrication of qualifications. Sometimes job applicants provide false or misleading information hoping it will help them secure the desired job. But this is a dangerous path to take, according to a survey of hiring managers conducted by CareerBuilder. com. The survey found that 57% of hiring managers have found a lie on a candidate's application, even though only 5% of applicants admit to such falsifications. In nearly all cases, the applicant did not get hired as a result of falsifying his or her résumé.

Obviously, you don't want to damage your chances of securing that coveted career position. To summarize, avoid these mistakes:

- Typos, inaccuracies, and lies
- Poor or no formatting—small or mixed fonts (smaller than size 10), odd margins
- Chunky paragraphs that are hard to read, or no bullet points
- Inappropriate content—from e-mail and Web addresses to irrelevant jobs and personal details
- Too much creativity—cute graphics, scented or funny-textured paper, photos or other over-the-top means of standing out from the crowd
- Lack of focus, or no clear objective or reason for applying for the specific job opening

---

Which of the items on this list might you have included before reading this section?

_____

_____

_____

_____

Scannable and Video Résumés

> **KEY POINT**
>
> Keywords are required if your résumé will be scanned or digitized.

Some companies rely on scanning software to pre-screen job applicants. These programs rely on keyword filters. Keywords are usually nouns that the company has identified as relevant to its needs. If you send your résumé to a company that uses such software, your document should contain keywords from the position announcement to help you pass the initial scan. However, don't fabricate or over-state your keyword qualifications because a human reviewer eventually will read your résumé and can see through such attempts to fool the software.

Video résumés are another matter altogether. For the on-campus recruitment process, a video résumé is unnecessary. However, online job posting sites do accept such files; and in some industries, such as theatre or the arts, they can be an effective way of visually presenting your qualifications and portfolio. Do some research before embarking on such a venture because a cheesy or amateurish video résumé can backfire and might even end up on YouTube as an example of what NOT to do!

> Of the companies you are interested in working for, which require or accept these résumé formats?
>
> _____
> _____
> _____
> _____

What Employers Say

KEY POINT

Strong oral and written communication abilities top the list of soft skills recruiters seek in job candidates.

Regardless of the position you seek, most employers are looking to hire candidates who demonstrate the ability to think analytically and apply quantitative problem-solving skills to the tasks at hand. For nearly every industry, strong oral and written communication skills actually top the list, along with the ability to work with—and lead—others in accomplishing work tasks. Your cover letter and résumé provide evidence that you possess these soft skills. We'll address each of these skill sets in later projects. But if you can strengthen your résumé by listing your own abilities in these areas, be sure to include them.

> What strengths do you have in the above noted areas?
>
> _____
> _____
> _____
> _____

The Cover Letter

KEY POINT

The goal of the cover letter is to get the reader to look at your résumé.

With your résumé complete, it's time to write your cover letter. Think of the cover letter as a summary of your interests and qualifications. This is your first chance to sell yourself and hook the reader so he or she will want to meet you. The contents must be perfect—no typos or strange phrases that you wouldn't use in real life. Jill Tanner's cover letter is shown in Figure 1-4. As you can see, a simple and clean format makes it easy to read quickly.

Figure 1-4	Example of a cover letter

Jill Tanner
15066 McConnell Circle
Reno, Nevada 89509
(775) 555-1445
jtanner@ureno.edu

September 15, 2012

Mr. Ben Shuman
Manager, Human Resources
Paramount Investment Corp.
45 South Virginia Lane
Reno, Nevada 89519

Dear Mr. Shuman:

I am applying for the investment analyst position that was advertised this week in the placement office at the University of Reno. Based upon my education and background, I believe I am a good fit for this position.

The position announcement indicates you are seeking a team player with excellent analytical, oral, and written communication skills and a B.S. degree in Business, with an emphasis in Accounting or Finance. I plan to graduate in December with a B.S. degree in Finance from the University of Reno. In addition, I have held a part-time job as a customer service representative with e-Vestments, a local investment company specializing in real estate ventures, for the past two years and found this position ideal for honing my understanding of financial markets and investments.

My finance courses in investing, financial analysis, working capital management, and real estate finance have taught me valuable industry-related skills. These skills include researching personal investment strategies; analyzing personal retirement portfolios to balance risk and return; analyzing pro-forma financial statements for decision making; managing assets for small businesses; and applying principles of rate of return, taxation, appraisal, and financing options to real estate investments.

I'm confident I have the requisite skills and background to make a contribution to your company's success, and am excited about the prospect of using my education and experience to the benefit of Paramount Investment Corp.

If you think I'm the candidate you are seeking to fill this position, or would like more information, I may be reached at (775) 555-1445 or via e-mail at jtanner@ureno.edu. Thank you for your consideration.

Sincerely,

Jill Tanner

Jill Tanner

KEY POINT

Address your cover letter to the company recruiter, not "To whom it may concern."

One of the most common mistakes people make on their cover letters is not addressing the letter to anyone in particular. A letter addressed "Dear Sir or Madam" or "To Whom It May Concern" tells the reader you didn't care enough to find out who would be reviewing your correspondence. That's not the first impression you want to make! So do a little digging into the company's Web site or simply call the company's main telephone number to find out who the human resources director is, or the name of the person doing the hiring.

In the opening sentence, indicate the position you are applying for and where you learned about it. Then provide some indication that you have reviewed the qualifications and believe you are the right person for the position.

> Write a sample opening sentence for your cover letter here.
>
> _____
> _____
> _____
> _____

In the body of the letter, summarize your qualifications—a bulleted list works well for this—to make it easy for the reader to see why you might be a good fit for the position. By doing a good job here, the reader will want to review the details of your résumé and contact you for an interview. That's your goal!

> List your key qualifications here.
>
> _____
> _____
> _____
> _____

At the end, you can also indicate that you will follow up in a short period of time—say, a week or so—to schedule an interview. Don't be shy about calling if you really want the job. Most employers value applicants who follow up, even if there are no job openings. But be careful—calling more than once a week can be annoying and may disqualify you from the running when there is an opening in the future. Also, resist the temptation to have your parents do the follow-up for you. That's a sure sign that you're not yet ready for a professional career.

Finally, close the letter by thanking the reader for considering you for an interview and sign your name.

Making a Good First Impression

The Interview

Congratulations! Your résumé got you an interview, but it won't get you the job. You now need to spend some time preparing for the interview.

If you haven't already researched the company, you should do so now. The Internet makes it easy to do basic research. At a minimum, use a search engine such as Bing or Google to locate the company's official Web site. Read about its products and services, locations, and press releases. Review the posted financial information for investors to gain a sense of the company's size and markets. That basic accounting class you took will come in handy here. Then expand your search to other online news articles: Who are the company's competitors, what effect is the economy having on the industry, and what are the company's growth potential or international expansion plans? If you know the names of the people who will be interviewing you, locate their profiles in professional social media sites, such as LinkedIn, and add what you find to your other research findings to demonstrate that you really do have an interest in working with them and the company.

Next, practice your responses to interview questions. Some sample interview questions are listed in Figure 1-5. Ask your school's placement office for some examples or locate some sample sets on the Web by conducting a search for "job interview questions." You won't be asked all of these questions, but you must be prepared to respond quickly, succinctly, and honestly to any question you are asked. Participate in **mock interviews** at your school, if they're offered. A mock interview is an interview conducted for practice. If your mock interview is videotaped, even better! It will be difficult to watch yourself, but the feedback can help you correct mistakes you don't want to make when the real interview takes place. Recruiters say this always helps to prepare candidates for the real thing because they get a chance to practice without penalty and receive valuable feedback on strengths and weaknesses.

Figure 1-5	**Sample interview questions**

Sample behavioral interview questions

Tell me about a time you worked on a team. How did it go?	Describe a recent failure you experienced. What did you learn from it, and what would you do differently next time?
Describe a time when you had a disagreement with someone at work or on a team. How did you handle and resolve the conflict?	Tell me about the last opportunity you had to set a goal and work toward it.
Tell me about a time when you used your ability to persuade others. What approach worked for you?	When did you last prepare a detailed written report? What was it, and how did you accomplish this task?
Describe how you manage many different priorities and deadlines. When was the last time you had to do this, and how did it go?	Tell me about a time when you demonstrated leadership ability.
Tell me about a time when you used your logic and problem-solving ability.	Describe a recent experience with making a presentation to influence someone's opinion.

Sample traditional interview questions

Tell me about yourself. Or, how would you describe yourself?	How has college prepared you for a career with (name of company)?
What influenced you to choose this career?	Tell me about your accomplishments. Which one are you the proudest of achieving? Why?
What do you see yourself doing in five years? Ten years?	What does success mean to you, and how do you know when you've achieved it?
If you had a "do over" for something in the past, what would it be?	In which area of our company are you most interested in working?
Given the investment (name of company) will make in your training and career, why should we hire you over other candidates for this position?	What is your biggest weakness?

When your research is finished, come up with two or three questions you can ask at the end of your interview. Most recruiters allow time at the end for you to do this. If you don't have any questions, the recruiter will think that you aren't that interested in the position or that you haven't done your homework before the meeting. Just be sure the questions focus on the company and the position—not vacation time or salary.

Think about your future career. List two or three questions you might ask a recruiter during your next interview that will demonstrate your interest in the position and company.

_____

_____

_____

_____

As you scan the interview questions in Figure 1-5 or those you found in your research, you might note that some of them ask for descriptive information, such as "Tell me what you did at Job X last summer." Others are more situation-based. This is a type of interview technique called **behavioral interviewing**, which involves asking candidates about how they reacted to or handled past situations or events. It is the preferred approach on college campuses today. In this case, the interviewer wants to hear how you behaved in a particular situation. For example, if the interviewer asks how you handled an angry customer or how you handled failure, he or she wants to know how you might respond when such a situation arises in the future. Be prepared to answer questions about how you identified a problem, worked on a team, resolved conflict, developed solutions, selected the best one, and implemented that choice.

Some sample behavioral interview questions you found online include:

_____

_____

_____

_____

Of course, you may still get some traditional interview questions, so be sure to think about—and practice!—how you'll respond if asked. For example, you might be asked to tell the interviewer about yourself. A short, one- or two-minute summary including your business-related experiences and personal accomplishments is expected and demonstrates that you've given thought to this type of broad opening question.

Your Appearance

You're probably familiar with the phrase, "a picture is worth a thousand words." The theory behind this statement also applies to you and your appearance. That's because how you look is the picture you present to the world every day. When it comes to preparing for your job search and interviews, the image presented by your résumé is only part of your picture. How you look and present yourself can further strengthen the positive first impression you made with your résumé and cover letter.

To complicate matters, when you do get that important face-to-face interview, you only have a few minutes to make a good first impression, according to some studies. So getting your appearance right is critical if the picture you want to present is an accurate reflection of who you are. Hiring managers are not shy about revealing what makes an impression—good or bad. "A suit jacket and tie are essential for men," says one major corporate recruiter from the Southwest. "That first impression tells me how serious you are about working for my company." Another recruiter adds, the applicant should "Look me in the eye and shake my hand with a smile. This is a great way to start off the interview."

The guidelines given here aren't set in stone. For example, if you're applying for a creative position where nobody dresses in suits, then a more casual approach to interview attire is fine. Do some research ahead of time so you don't make the wrong impression at the interview. Call the human resources department of the company or seek advice from the career counselors at your school if you're not sure. Often, the attire worn to the interview is expected to be more formal even if the workplace is casual. Your goal is to underscore your competence and professionalism by your appearance. It's better to be over-dressed and taken seriously than to be disqualified for the position because of your appearance.

If you think these guidelines are too picky, remember that the job market is competitive. If you don't follow the guidelines, others still will. You'll make the recruiter's job of eliminating you as a candidate much easier if you don't pay attention to the impression you make. As you read the following guidelines, take a look at Figure 1-6 for an example of appropriate attire for both men and women.

What type of dress code does your chosen career have? How does that translate into what you should wear to the interview?

_____

_____

_____

_____

Figure 1-6   **Examples of business attire**

Yuri Arcurs/Shutterstock.com, iofoto/Shutterstock.com, and Yuri Arcurs/Shutterstock.com

Impression #1: Attire

Men:

- Clean suit, shirt, and silk tie in a conservative pattern (no jeans or casual sweaters, no ties with questionable graphics or sports team logos, and no bow ties or clip-ons)
- Belt that coordinates with suit (black belt with black or gray suit, for example)
- Socks that match your pants (not white)
- Dress shoes—polished with heels that are not worn down (no sport shoes, white socks, or athletic gear)

Women:

- Clean suit—skirts no shorter than an inch above the knee; depending on the job, nice slacks (never jeans) may be OK if common for the industry
- Blouse that is not too low cut and doesn't have gaps between the buttons when you move (bend over and stretch your arms back to test)
- Neutral undergarments and hosiery—no patterns or holes
- Heels 2½ inches high or less, closed toe and heel, color should match outfit; no strappy evening wear (peep toe shoes may be OK to wear on the job, but not to the interview)
- Conservative make-up with neutral colors—natural-looking and no sparkles

Both:

- Pressed and clean clothing; no stains, tears, patches, or missing buttons
- Empty pockets to avoid bulges or jingling change or keys (put all of this in your portfolio or briefcase)
- No lace, ruffles, or shiny fabrics
- Avoid clingy knits or anything too revealing
- Colors—black, gray, navy (solid color or subtle stripe OK)
- Briefcase or portfolio instead of backpack and purse, with résumé and reference copies, portfolio samples, or other materials
- No flip-flops or casual sandals

Impression #2: Appearance and Grooming

- Shower, use deodorant, and brush your teeth the day of the interview; consider brushing your teeth and using breath mints right before the interview if you had garlic or other strong flavors for lunch
- No colognes or perfumes, as some people are allergic
- Smokers—minimize exposure to smoke before the interview so you don't carry a cloud with you into the room
- No chewing gum, candy, or tobacco products
- Neat haircut, not over-styled; natural color (not purple, pink, or green)
- Freshly shaved face for men—moustaches and beards are sometimes considered negative for new employees, but check your industry
- Cover tattoos and remove piercings (especially tongue, lip, nose, eyebrow); earrings are OK for women but not more than one per ear
- Fingernails clean and hands scrubbed; natural nails, clear polish, or French manicure for women—no piercings or appliqués
- Remove excessive jewelry—leave the bling at home; men: dress watch, wedding or class ring only, no earrings; women: dress watch, necklace, and one pair of earrings to coordinate with outfit; no sport watches, only one ring per hand on ring finger (no thumb rings)

Impression #3: Technology

- Turn off your cell phone during the interview; wait until you are out of the building to make calls or send text messages
- Leave the MP3 player and earphones in your briefcase, in your car, or at home

---

Make this list your personal interview checklist. Which of these tips did you not know before reading this section?

_____

_____

_____

_____

Some Tips for the Big Day

- When you go to the interview, be sure to show up five to 10 minutes early. Allow yourself plenty of time to get to the interview location, park, and locate the office. Visit the restroom to check your appearance, wash your hands, and touch up your hair and make-up—don't groom in the lobby! Why? The office receptionist may be asked what kind of first impression you made when you entered the office, so the impression you make here counts, too. Be polite and respectful to the receptionist because you must interact with him or her in order to meet with the interviewer; and if you land the job, you also will work with this person later on.

- Bring a small briefcase or folio containing a couple of pens, a pad of paper, extra copies of your résumé, and a few copies of your reference list, in case the interviewer requests them. If a portfolio of work projects is essential to the interview, make sure the folio and the work inside are organized, clean, and neat.

- When you meet the interviewer, stand up straight, smile, look the person in the eye, and extend your right hand to shake the person's hand. A quick but firm shake is all that is required. There is no need to pump your arm or squeeze the person's hand too hard.

- When you sit down, place your briefcase or portfolio next to you on the floor. Place your hands in your lap; and if you must cross your legs, do so at the ankle. Avoid swinging crossed legs while seated to minimize distraction.

- Be sure to have two or three questions prepared to ask the interviewer—something you discovered about the company while conducting your research, questions about the company's employee performance review process or telecommuting policies, or a comment about a recent news event that affects the company. Has it recently expanded overseas? If so, what does that mean for the company's future growth? Keep it upbeat yet demonstrate that you have done your homework. If nothing else, ask about the next steps in the interview process, or when you might expect to hear back about the position. If you don't have any questions, the message you send to the recruiter is that you really aren't that interested in the job.

What are some good questions to ask at the end of an interview?

_____

_____

_____

_____

- As the interviewer signals the end of the interview, stand up and shake the interviewer's hand again. It's acceptable to ask about the next steps in the interview process and when you can expect to hear back from the company about the position. Reiterate your interest in the position. Be sure to thank the interviewer for his or her time. Ask for a business card so you'll have the correct contact information when sending your thank you note.

The Thank You Note

The interview is over; you did everything correctly. The job should be yours, right? Not so fast. You still have one more task to complete—a thank you note. Whether it's typed or handwritten, a note sent to the interviewer within 24 hours of the interview helps to round out the great first impression you made in person. It demonstrates that you know more about business relationships and communication than what's written on the résumé and that you are serious about wanting the job. If more than one person interviewed you, then send each one a note.

According to Katharine Hansen at QuintCareers.com, only about 5% of people seeking jobs follow up with a thank you note after the interview. Do you see the opportunity to set yourself apart here? If the company culture is more formal, send a typed note. If it's more casual, or if you had a special rapport with the interviewer, consider sending a handwritten note if your handwriting is nice. Jill Tanner's thank you note, which is included in Figure 1-7, is a good example of what to include. Be sure to personalize your thank you note by commenting on something the interviewer said that was meaning-ful to you or a key qualification you discussed that you want to reinforce. And, just like your résumé and cover letter, be sure to proofread it so it's free of typos and grammatical errors. After all, this is one more chance to sell yourself and help seal the deal.

Figure 1-7	Sample thank you note

Jill Tanner
15066 McConnell Circle
Reno, Nevada 89509
(775) 555-1445
jtanner@ureno.edu

October 1, 2012

Mr. Ben Shuman
Manager, Human Resources
Paramount Investment Corp.
45 South Virginia Lane
Reno, Nevada 89519

Dear Mr. Shuman:

Thank you for meeting with me today to discuss the career opportunities at your firm. As we discussed, my educational background and work experience seem to be a good fit for the entry-level investment analyst position at Paramount Investment Corp., and I look forward to contributing to the company's future success.

As mentioned in the interview, I can bring a fresh perspective to your work environment from my recent experience as a business analyst at the Small Business Administration. Working with potential new small business owners has really given me a good understanding of how important solid investment research and advice can be to clients as they build their businesses. I'm also looking forward to applying the knowledge gained in my college coursework to real client situations and helping clients realize their financial goals.

I appreciate the time you took to meet with me today. I remain very interested in working for you and look forward to hearing from you soon about this position.

Sincerely,

Jill Tanner

Jill Tanner

What about an e-mail thank you? There are mixed feelings among company recruiters on this point. If the company culture relies heavily on e-mail for communication—and you've been corresponding with the company in this fashion already—then a quick e-mail message might be fine. But be sure to also follow up with a paper note. There are plenty of good thank you note examples online. So if the one in Figure 1-7 doesn't quite work for you, take a look at some online samples to help craft one that better suits your style. Thinking of sending a text message thank you? Don't. Old-school written notes are still best.

It's perfectly acceptable to follow up with a company if you haven't heard anything after a couple of weeks. Eighty-two percent of companies expect to be contacted, according to a Robert Half International survey. Just be careful not to contact the company too frequently or you might end up ruining your good first impression by being perceived as over-eager or a pest.

Reasons People Don't Get Job Offers

Aside from not following the advice provided in this workbook, there are other reasons people don't get hired. As you look over Figure 1-8, you'll see that some of them are pretty obvious but others are more subtle. Use this list to make sure you avoid mistakes.

Figure 1-8 | **Common reasons people don't get job offers**

Poor personal hygiene or appearance	Negative attitude about past employers or work assignments	Lack of genuine interest in employer
Overly aggressive or arrogant	Lack of enthusiasm, confidence or poise	No eye contact
Late for interview	More interested in money than position	Unwilling to start at the bottom
Unrealistic salary or benefits expectations	Carelessness on resume and other correspondence	Failure to ask questions during the interview
Lack of tact, maturity or courtesy	No sense of humor	Inability to answer questions clearly

Technology Skills—Working with Templates in Word 2010

Microsoft provides a variety of templates on Office.com for creating professional-looking résumés quickly. By using a predesigned format, you can focus on filling in your specific information and rest assured that the layout will be viewed favorably when read. You must be connected to the Internet to access these resources.

The Technology Skills steps cover these skills:

- Download a résumé template on Office.com.
- Create your own personalized résumé for an entry-level position.

To download a résumé template on Office.com:

1. Open Word 2010.

2. Click **File>New**. The New Document window opens with Available and Office.com template sections. See Figure 1-9.

Figure 1-9 **Word templates**

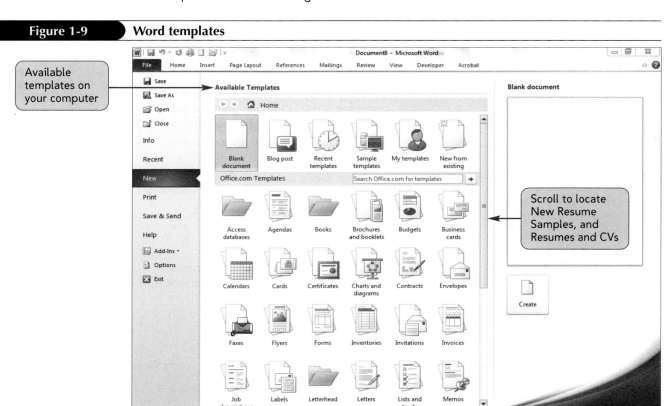

Available templates on your computer

Scroll to locate New Resume Samples, and Resumes and CVs

3. Scroll through the available templates found under the Office.com heading and look for "New Resume Samples" and "Resumes and CVs." The "New Resume Samples" link offers résumé templates for defined career positions that are already filled in.

4. Find the template that best suits your style and then click on it to download it. For most entry-level positions, this will be a chronological résumé format.

5. Fill in the placeholders with your information. Be sure to follow the detailed guidelines in this project when deciding what content to include.

6. Delete any extra placeholders so they don't appear in your résumé.

7. Save your completed résumé using the file name **(Your Name)_OnlineResume'.docx**.

To add résumé information to an offline template:

If you want to prepare a chronological résumé but don't have access to the Internet, use the résumé template provided with this workbook. This file is very basic but is a good start for preparing a professional-looking résumé.

To start, follow these steps:

> **1.** Open the file **Resume_Template_01.docx** located in the Project.01 folder included with your Data Files, and then, to avoid altering the original file, save the document as **(Your Name)_Resume.docx** on your local drive or other storage location.

> **2.** Fill in the placeholders with your information using the guidelines in this project.

> **3.** Delete any extra placeholders so they don't appear in your résumé.

> **4.** Save your complete résumé.

TIP

Click the Page Layout tab in the Themes group to dress up a basic résumé layout.

Your Cover Letter and Thank You Note

After completing the Technology Skills résumé project, use the information and Web resources from this project to prepare your cover letter and thank you note. Start files for both of these documents are provided in the Project.01 folder. The start files are titled **Practice_01.docx** and **Practice_02.docx**.

To complete the cover letter:

1. Open the **Practice_01.docx** Word document, located in the Project.01 folder included with your Data Files, and then, to avoid altering the original file, save the document as **(Your Name)_CoverLetter.docx** on your local drive or other storage location.

2. Enter your name and personal contact information in the placeholder at the top of the document.

3. Replace the placeholder for today's date with the date of the letter.

4. Replace the company contact information with the name and address of the person who will be reviewing your résumé.

5. Insert the name of the recruiter or human resources contact in the salutation.

6. In the first paragraph, insert the name of the position you are seeking, and specify where you heard about the job posting.

7. In the second paragraph, insert your education and other qualifications for the position. Insert your graduation date, degree, major or emphasis, school name, and work experiences in lieu of the placeholders.

8. In the third paragraph, insert the name of your field in both locations, and add your skills that relate to the position in that field.

9. Replace the placeholder in paragraph four with the name of the company.

10. Insert your telephone number and e-mail address in the last paragraph.

11. Delete the note under "Sincerely" that reminds you to sign your letter, and replace "Your name" with your full name.

12. Save your letter.

13. Print your letter and sign it before sending it with your résumé.

To complete the thank you note:

1. Open the **Practice_02.docx** Word document located in the Project.01 folder included with your Data Files, and then, to avoid altering the original file, save the document as **(Your Name)_ThankYouNote.docx** on your local drive or other storage location.

2. Enter your name and personal contact information in the placeholder at the top of the document.

3. Replace the placeholder for today's date with the date of the letter.

4. Replace the company contact information with the name and address of the person who interviewed you. Use the business card you obtained at the interview to be sure you have the correct address and spelling of the recruiter's name. If you had interviews with more than one person, write each person a thank you note.

5. In the salutation, insert the name of the person who interviewed you.

6. In the first paragraph, insert the name of the position you interviewed for.

7. In the second paragraph, replace all of the placeholders with your recent work experience, a description of how your work experience has prepared you for the job you are applying for, something about the position you discovered during the interview, and a description of what you hope to achieve as part of the organization.

8. Remove the placeholder for your signature, and save your letter.

9. Print your thank you note, sign it, and send it.

To print an envelope:

1. In Word, click the **Mailings** tab.

2. Click **Envelopes** in the Create group. The Envelopes and Labels pop-up box will appear (Figure 1-10).

Figure 1-10   **Printing an envelope**

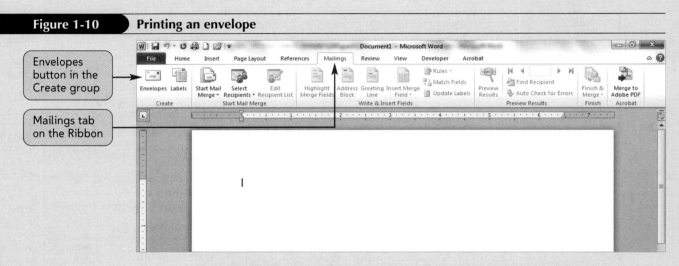

3. Enter the mailing address for the recipient in the Delivery address box. Put the recipient's name, with title (Mrs., Mr., etc.), on the first line. Put the company name on the second line. Put the address on the third line, and the city, state, and zip or postal code on the last line (Figure 1-11).

Figure 1-11   **The envelopes and labels dialog box**

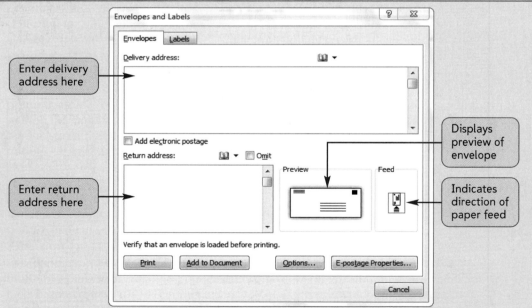

4. Enter your name and full address in the Return address box. Put your name on the first line, your address on the second line, and your city, state, and zip or postal code on the last line.

5. Follow the on-screen instructions for inserting a legal size envelope in your printer, and click **Print**.

Interview Preparation Checklist

REVISE

During your job search, you'll likely be interviewed by more than one company. To help keep track of which tasks you've completed for each organization, use the **Revise_01.docx** document to keep everything organized.

1. Open **Revise_01.docx**, located in the Project.01 folder included with your Data Files, and then, to avoid altering the original file, save the document as **(Your Name)_InterviewChecklist.docx** on your local drive or other storage location.

2. Save a copy for each company you'll be interviewing with. Name each copy as follows: **(CompanyName)_InterviewChecklist.docx**.

3. On the first form, fill in the name of the company, interview date, time and location, and name of the interviewer at the top. Repeat for each additional company.

4. Save and print a copy of the checklist for each company.

5. As you complete the checklist items for each company, fill in the date on the checklist. You can do this on paper or in your saved document.

List of Potential Interview Questions

CREATE

To help prepare for your upcoming interviews, you'll need to practice your responses to common interview questions so you are prepared with solid answers. In addition to the sample interview questions in Figure 1-5, conduct an online search to add questions to the list.

1. Open a Web browser, such as Internet Explorer, Safari, or Firefox.

2. Go to bing.com or google.com.

3. Search for "common interview questions" or "behavioral interview questions." As you type, search suggestions will appear below the search box. If any of those suggestions appeals to you, click on it to use it for your search.

4. Click the links for Web sites offering question and answer lists. Read or print the contents to locate the interview questions.

5. Watch a few of the video links that offer advice on interviews to pick up additional tips.

6. Prepare a list of interview questions and responses by copying and pasting the questions from the site to a new Word document. Fill in your own responses. Alternatively, make hand-written flashcards to use for practice.

7. Save and print your questions and responses as **(YourName)_InterviewQuestions.docx**.

Case Study 1

Encore Consulting, Part 1   Watch the Project 1 video episode 1a, "The Interview." Based on what you learned in this project, critique each student's preparation. If required by your instructor, fill in the **VideoCritique_Worksheet_01.docx** with your answers; and then save, print, and submit it.

1. **Matthew Brady**
   Things done well:

   _____
   _____
   _____
   _____

   Where he went wrong:

   _____
   _____
   _____
   _____

   Do you think he will be offered a job? Why or why not?

   _____
   _____
   _____
   _____

2. **Jill Tanner**
   Things done well:

   _____
   _____
   _____
   _____

   Where she went wrong:

   _____
   _____
   _____
   _____

   Do you think she will be offered a job? Why or why not?

   _____
   _____
   _____
   _____

3. **Sophie Aguilar**
   Things done well:

   _____
   _____
   _____
   _____

Where she went wrong:

_____

_____

_____

_____

Do you think she will be offered a job? Why or why not?

_____

_____

_____

_____

What specific actions will you take to prepare for your own job search and interviews?

_____

_____

_____

_____

What would you have done differently if you were interviewing for a position with Encore?

_____

_____

_____

_____

What mistakes might you have made if you hadn't read this chapter and watched the video?

_____

_____

_____

_____

Encore Consulting, Part 2   Next, watch the Video Episode 1b, "Good Interview." On the worksheet, write down the key actions from this project that are demonstrated in the interview. What did Tony do well?

Key actions:

_____

_____

_____

_____

Case Study 2

RESEARCH

Career Research: Online Company News and Current Events   As noted in this project, it's not enough to simply apply for a position and show up for the interview. The interviewers you meet will expect you to do your homework on their company! In fact, one common interview question is to ask you what you already know about the company. So, to help you prepare, follow these steps:

1. Open a Web browser, such as Internet Explorer, Safari, or Firefox.
2. Enter the company's Web address and navigate to its site. If you don't know it, use bing.com or google.com to search for the company name. The search results usually yield the link to the company's official Web site near the top of the results list.

3. Spend some time exploring the links for investor relations, press releases, and company info. There may be additional links to explore, as well.

4. Click on the Bing or Google news, photos, and video links to locate news stories, images, and videos.

5. Open a new Word document and record your findings. Cut and paste any news stories or other clippings of interest into your document.

6. Underneath each clipping, write a question or comment about the news stories that you could use during your interview to demonstrate that you've done your online research and taken more than a passing interest in the company.

7. Save your document as **(CompanyName)_Research.docx**.

8. Print a copy to bring to the interview so you have something to review while waiting to be called for your meeting.

Case Study 3

APPLY

Career Center Research There are numerous career resources available online and through your school. These resources can help you prepare your job search documents (résumé, cover letter, and thank you notes), practice interview questions, and research companies online. You've already explored some of the online resources; now take the time to get acquainted with your school's Career Services or Placement Center.

1. Locate the Career Services or Placement Center on your campus by asking your instructor or searching your school's Web site.

2. Obtain the office phone number and call to schedule an appointment to meet with a career advisor, if available. Alternatively, stop by the office to make the appointment in person.

3. Visit the office to learn more about its services. Some of the offerings might include mock interviews, computers connected to the Internet for conducting company research, print materials to help you prepare for interviews, and sample résumé copies.

4. Open a blank Word document. Type a summary of the findings from your visit.

5. Save your document as **(YourName)_CareerCenterResearch.docx**.

Your Online Brand

OBJECTIVES
- Manage your online brand
- Distinguish between appropriate and compromising online content
- Protect your personal privacy
- Secure your online information to avoid identity theft

Introduction

The information you choose to convey to the world about yourself during a job search is no longer limited to what's included on your résumé. What you voluntarily post about yourself on the Internet—part of your online brand—is a natural extension of the image you present to the public.

Ranked among the top Web sites people visit regularly, social networks such as Facebook, LinkedIn, and China's Renren have become some of the Internet's fastest-growing entities. Starting from nothing in 2003, they have become the daily points of connection, communication, and community for hundreds of millions of people around the world. Personal data, photos, videos, messages, and more fill personal pages as people document their lives online. Blogs and wikis also have found a home as more people choose to digitally express themselves on the Internet.

With around-the-clock access to this personal information, questions related to both appropriateness and privacy have started to surface. Although you might post photos and comments online to keep your friends and family informed, companies have used these same postings as a rich source of information, giving them a more complete picture of who you are and how you are likely to behave as an employee. The line between what is considered private information and what is considered fair game by employers has become blurred. Knowing how to best manage your online brand has never been more important or relevant.

STARTING DATA FILES

Project.02

Tech_02.docx
Revise_02.docx
Create_02.docx
VideoCritique_Worksheet_02.docx

Encore Consulting: Video Episode 2

In the Project 1 Encore Video Episodes 1a and 1b, you watched four student candidates—Matthew, Jill, Sophie, and Tony—going through on-campus interviews with Candace Johnson and Gerry West, the recruiters from Encore. The candidates exhibited varying states of preparedness, which you critiqued for use in your own career preparation activities.

Our story picks up here in Episode 2 with Candace coming back to the office to review interview results from a number of colleges. Watch Candace's introduction on the video that accompanies this text, and then read what happened back at the office in the section below.

Scenario—Encore corporate headquarters, Candace Johnson's office

Candace: "Over the past couple of weeks, I've interviewed dozens of students at several schools in the region, as has my colleague, Gerry. Now, I'm back in the office to determine who will get called for a second interview here at our office. Some of the candidates were well prepared, which definitely gives them an advantage. But there's some homework I need to do before we extend offers for visits."

Candace and her assistant, Fermina, begin poring over the interview notes and résumés collected during the recruiting run. Fifteen students were interviewed. Candace creates a quick summary of her observations from the first few.

Candace: "Let's review Sophie Aguilar's résumé and interview. Her appearance was the first sign she might not be a good fit for our firm. She was slightly disheveled and wore excessive jewelry—although her suit was OK, if a bit bright in color. I wonder if she looked in the mirror before she left the house! Can you imagine what one of our clients would think? She needs to exude professionalism and competence. And wrong as it may seem, she will be judged on her appearance—which will initially affect how much the client will respect her work. She also didn't seem to have done any research or have any idea of the type of work we do—not a good sign."

"Now, as for Matthew Brady, it's clear his mother is controlling his actions. Although I'm supportive of being close to family, he's an adult who now needs to take charge of his own affairs. We've had enough situations involving parents calling Human Resources when they don't think their child has received a fair raise or promotion, or been given a decent job assignment. In addition, he gave some signals by his answers that he isn't interested in a long-term career with Encore. What did he say? Oh, yes: *'A job like this could be a good place to start for a year or two before I move on to something else.'* With a short-term attitude, he'd not likely pay attention to details or fully engage in the continuing education we require. He *was* dressed well, though, but I suspect that was mom's doing and not his own. We need people who can think and act for themselves."

"Now, as for Jill Tanner, she made a good first impression on me. Her résumé was impeccable, and it was clear from the questions she asked that she had done her homework on Encore. She looked me in the eye and had a good firm handshake, too, which will impress our clients. The only thing we'll need to work on is her definition of professional attire. Although her suit was nice, the skirt was too short and the open-toe, strappy heels are not appropriate for the work world. We've seen this before, though, with college students. With a little side discussion about professional attire, she should be just fine. I'd like to invite her in for a second interview to meet the rest of our team, so they can provide their evaluation of her as a potential colleague. They trust me to check out the education and work experience qualifications—all the items on the résumé—so they're going to look for personality fit and interests, and whether they could spend an hour in the car with her while driving to the client location. This will be our chance to sell her on Encore as the best place to start her career at the same time. After all, we do much of our work in groups; so if she meets with their approval and she likes what she sees, we could be extending an offer within a couple weeks."

"Gerry has forwarded information on a student named Tony Bonacci that he interviewed last week. Let's see…his recruiting summary indicates the following: pleasant demeanor and good handshake, a bit quiet or shy, well-dressed, shoes polished, clean fingernails, and neatly cut hair. And a portfolio with Excel spreadsheet assignment projects! Good, good…strong résumé with several teamwork experiences and even some leadership. Gerry doesn't say whether he sent a thank you note, but everything else looks favorable."

As Candace finishes reviewing the rest of the résumés and interview notes, Fermina hands her the day's mail. She also gives Candace the results of her informal, online checks of each candidate.

Candace: "Here's a nice thank you note from Sophie. It is handwritten, which is fine, and well written. I also see an e-mail follow-up note from her, asking when her office visit and second interview will be since she's really busy this semester and might not have time if we wait too long. Hmmm…."

"I see I've also received a handwritten thank you note from Matthew. But it looks like mom's handwriting."

"I don't see anything yet from Jill, though. That's a bit disappointing, since she was on the right track up to this point. It would have moved her to the top of the candidate second interview list if she had followed up, but the fact that she didn't will not completely ruin her chances."

"As for the online search results, it would appear that none of the candidates bothered to clean up their social network pages. It's OK to have a personal life, but I'd rather not see our employees posting pictures of themselves drinking, or scantily clad. If a client saw these images, it might compromise the integrity of the employee and give the client a reason to question that employee's judgment in a professional situation. In fact, we had an incident last year with one of our consultants that put us in a sticky situation and we ended up having to terminate her employment. We don't need that headache again!"

After finishing her review, Candace says, "OK, that's what I needed to make my final recommendations for second interviews."

Social Networks, Blogs, Wiki Postings, and Your Career

With the rapid growth of social networks on the Internet, the line between your personal life and public life is sometimes difficult to distinguish. A **social network** is a Web site that allows individuals to connect with others. Users can post photo, video, audio, and text content about themselves on custom-created digital pages, and then create a network of friends linked through each other's pages. Blogs and wikis also are rich sources of information, posted by individuals who wish to use the Internet as their soapbox or simply to exercise their First Amendment rights to free speech. A **blog** is an online journal, usually written in chronological order by an individual. A **wiki** is a collaborative Web site that permits multiple users to edit or add content.

It may not seem fair that total strangers can (and do) look at what you have posted on a social network page, blog, or wiki and use it to judge you. Yet the very public nature of the Internet makes it easy to do. In fact, nearly eight out of 10 employers perform online searches to see what else they can learn about the people who have applied to work for them, according to the business social networking site ExecuNet. Surveys conducted by CareerBuilder.com and the National Association of Colleges and Employers have yielded similar results. Yet 60% of Internet users are not concerned about what others find, according to the Pew Internet Project, and most don't take steps to control what's out there. In fact, nearly 75% of users have only looked once or twice for their digital presence.

More than half of the companies surveyed by CareerBuilder.com eliminated a candidate because of information they found posted online. The information included questionable or inappropriate postings and photos, poor communication skills, links to criminal behavior, and lies about qualifications. And it's not limited to just a few social network sites. Employers also use Google, WebMii, and companies that specialize in background checks to search for job candidates. They may even take a look at YouTube.

An employer cannot ask questions about a person's social life during an interview, but there is no law prohibiting the discovery of his or her interests from online sources. The bottom line: If you do not want a potential employer to learn more than you want to reveal, remove any content you deem off-limits from all public online sources, or at least make your pages private or only available on password-protected sites. Keep in mind, however, this content may still be accessed if the background check is thorough, so there's not a 100% guarantee of confidentiality or privacy. Figure 2-1 lists a few personal items to consider keeping off the Web.

Figure 2-1	Information that shouldn't be posted online
Age or birth date	Political affiliation
Race	Sexual orientation
Religion	Social activities and photos that may be viewed negatively
Unprofessional screen names	Personal correspondence or postings intended only for friends and family

What online sites contain personal information, photos, or videos about you that may make a potential employer question your fit with the company? Consider the links to friends' pages and postings as well.

_____

_____

_____

_____

What items from Figure 2-1 should you consider removing from online sites that you don't want potential employers or future business colleagues to see?

_____

_____

_____

_____

What, exactly, are potential employers looking for in these online searches? In addition to learning more about your demographics and your social and personal interests, they're looking for signals that you'll be a valuable contributor to their enterprise. According to a survey by ERE Media, companies are looking for a wide range of attributes, as shown in Figure 2-2.

Figure 2-2	Attributes employers look for in online searches
1.	Résumé content verification: job skills, employment history, contact information
2.	Presentation and communication skills
3.	Integrity, intelligence, and good judgment
4.	Professionalism and club/association affiliations
5.	Creativity or ability to be innovative

In addition to informal online searches, many employers also rely on independent, third-party background checks to verify résumé claims and to uncover anything that may have been omitted. When such background checks are used, the Fair Credit Reporting Act (FCRA)—which regulates the collection, distribution, and use of consumer credit information—requires the employer to notify the applicant when negative information turns up, along with the name of the company that provided the information. To conduct background checks for certain information, such as driving, felony, or credit history, the applicant's written permission will be required. However, informal searches, such as a Google or WebMii search, do not fall under the requirements of the FCRA. The issue here for job applicants is that there is usually no opportunity to explain or defend the online information, or to correct it if the content contains material errors.

If you have any concerns about what your background check may reveal, consider paying the nominal fee charged by companies such as Spokeo, MyBackgroundCheck, and US Search so you can be prepared in case questions arise. Just what might show up? Anything you have been charged with—not just convictions—back to age 18 or 21, in some cases. There is no seven-year statute of limitations on what a background check can reveal; so if you have any driving violations, drug charges, or "minor in possession" citations, they could appear. If you do get questioned about your background by the recruiters, don't lie. Depending on the issue, if you are honest and direct with the company, chances are it won't be held against you in the hiring process.

Another possibility to consider is subscribing to an online service that will regularly scour the Internet on your behalf to locate information being posted about you. Such services search all social networks, professional review Web sites, blogs, online news sources, and digital media sharing sites, such as YouTube and Flickr, in addition to all publicly available Internet sites. One such company, Reputation.com, can even handle the dirty work of getting the negative or potentially damaging content removed.

Branding Yourself Online

KEY POINT

Regularly conducting online searches for your digital presence can minimize problems later on.

Does the growing use of online resources by recruiters mean you need to erase all digital evidence of your existence from the Internet? Not at all. That may send a negative signal as well. Instead, consider the content on the Internet as an extension of your résumé and manage it as your own personal marketing space.

Here are some ways to enhance what others may find when they search. First, clean up any postings you've made to social networking sites such as Facebook and MySpace, or delete (not just de-activate) any accounts you want to close. Remove any posted interests that would portray you as irresponsible or immature, including both text and photos. Consider paring back your list of friends, especially those whose online postings might contain photos of or content about you that you no longer want the public to see. You may even want to ask friends to remove photos of you that they have posted on their sites if you think the photos could be located.

Which friends do I need to ask to remove questionable images or comments about me?

_____

_____

_____

_____

Consider purchasing your own domain name through one of the Internet registrants, such as Network Solutions or Register.com. These sites show up in online searches and may prove valuable in countering any negative online content found by a potential employer. When you buy your own domain name, you can then create and post a Web site with positive content that you control. Think of it as your personal marketing space. As an alternative, create a simple Web site hosted by an Internet service provider or the free Google Sites (google.com/sites) that at least lets you control the content posted there.

Go to networksolutions.com or register.com and conduct a domain name search for your name. Is it available? How much does it cost? Does this seem like a good investment?

_____

_____

_____

_____

Do you like to write? Think about starting a blog that you can use to express your views at a site such as blogger.com, wordpress.com, or livejournal.com. Blog entries are "signed" by the author (you), so your blog should show up when an online search for your name is performed. Some recruiters are starting to use blog-searching tools such as Technorati, Blogdigger, and Daypop to review blog postings. Just make sure that the topics you discuss on any blog will be viewed favorably by a potential employer.

What about Twitter? This short-message service is increasingly being used to broadcast, or "tweet," to "followers" what you are up to, in real time and using only 140 characters. Companies are now using Twitter for business reasons, including tweets about open positions, so having a personal account is fine—but be sure your tweets, like your other online postings, tell a consistent and positive story about you. If you're interested in working for certain companies, be sure to follow them on Twitter so you get the latest news updates, including job postings, when they're sent. Who knows? Your next big job opportunity just might come to you this way.

Another way to demonstrate that you're serious about your professional career and online brand is to join a business-oriented social networking site, such as LinkedIn. Put it on your résumé, or mention it during the interview. Started in 2003, this network contains close to 100 million professionals around the world, including executives from all the Fortune 500 companies. Think of LinkedIn as a gigantic electronic address book. Corporate recruiters are starting to use this site not only to learn more about current job applicants, but also to find people who haven't applied but might be the right person for a job opening. According to LinkedIn cofounder Konstantin Guericke, well over 100,000 recruiters are registered on the site. There may be other networking sites associated with your chosen profession that you could join as well. Doing so can demonstrate that you are serious about joining the ranks of working professionals in your field. You can ask your instructors who are members to connect with you and provide recommendations, if appropriate. If you do join such a site, include keywords in your profile that describe you and will help someone find you when conducting a search. Some examples include the very words you used in your résumé.

Look at the résumé you created in Project 1. What keywords might be used to describe you in an online search?

_____

_____

_____

_____

Online Personal Privacy and Information Security

The use of online searches by corporate recruiters may be disturbing to some applicants, but the fact that an immense amount of personal information can be sourced electronically should not be a surprise to you. After all, much of that information has been openly and knowingly provided by you through Web sites, social networks, blog posts, and Twitter feeds. The challenge, as you've discovered earlier in the project, is managing the information that's available online. By remaining aware of potential uses and risks, employing common sense, and taking precautions, you can maintain a comfortable level of security and privacy. The following section discusses some laws, practices, and tools that can help.

Privacy Laws

Concerns about privacy have led to the enactment of federal and state laws regarding the storage and disclosure of personal data, as shown in Figure 2-3. There are several common threads connecting these laws. For example:

- Information collected and stored about individuals should be limited to what is necessary to carry out the function of the business or government agency collecting the data.
- Once collected, provisions should be made to restrict data access to only those employees within the organization who need such access to do their jobs.
- Personal information should be released outside the collecting organization only when the individual has agreed to its disclosure.
- When information is collected about an individual, that person should know that the data is being collected and have the chance to determine the accuracy of the data.

Figure 2-3	Selected U.S. Laws related to privacy

Date	Law	Purpose
2003	Fair and Accurate Credit Transactions Act of 2003 (FACT Act)	Allows consumers to put fraud alerts on their credit files if they believe they have been the victim of identity theft
2001; renewed 2006	Provide Appropriate Tools Required to Intercept and Obstruct Terrorism (PATRIOT) Act	Gives law enforcement the right to monitor people's activities, including Web and e-mail activity
1999	Gramm-Leach-Bliley Act (GLBA), also known as Financial Services Modernization Act	Protects individuals from unauthorized disclosures of financial information and requires entities to periodically report information disclosure policies to consumers
1996	National Information Infrastructure Protection Act	Penalizes theft of information across state lines, threats against networks, and computer system trespassing
1996	Health Insurance Portability and Accountability Act (HIPAA)	Regulates the disclosure of patient health information, requires providers to seek the patient's permission before sharing any medical or health-related information, and provides for the reporting of disclosed information to patients, upon request
1986	Electronic Communications Privacy Act (ECPA)	Provides the same right of privacy protection for the postal delivery service and telephone companies to the new forms of electronic communications, such as voice mail, e-mail, and cellular phones
1984	Computer Fraud and Abuse Act	Outlaws unauthorized access of federal government computers
1978	Right to Financial Privacy Act	Outlines procedures federal agencies must follow when looking at customer records in banks
1974	Privacy Act	Prohibits federal agencies from allowing information to be used for a reason other than that for which it was collected
1974	Family Educational Rights and Privacy Act (FERPA)	Gives students and parents access to school records and limits disclosure of records to unauthorized parties
1970	Fair Credit Reporting Act (FCRA)	Forbids credit reporting agencies from releasing credit information to unauthorized people and allows consumers to review their own credit records

It's important to note that although these laws provide legal protection to individuals, if you knowingly post or provide personal information for public display on Web sites such as social networks, such protection may no longer be afforded. Most Web sites now provide policy statements regarding the use of personal information. You should carefully review these statements before providing any personal information to Web sites.

Protecting Your Online Security and Privacy

KEY POINT

Actively engage in reading the privacy policies of the online resources you use.

As noted earlier, it's nearly impossible to keep personal information off the Internet. Instead, your goal should be to manage what is already available so that it can't be used in ways you never intended. In addition to using available security software and tools on your personal computer, you can also employ smart computing practices, such as limiting what you share online. Figure 2-4 outlines a few tips from the Electronic Frontier Foundation (EFF) for helping to maintain your personal privacy online.

Think for a moment about the Web sites where you may have entered personal information. Take a few minutes to read the posted privacy statements provided by each site's owner. What do their privacy policies reveal about how they use your information? If you are not comfortable with what you find, take steps now to remove the personal content.

_____

_____

_____

_____

_____

Figure 2-4	**Advice for protecting your online privacy**
Only provide information that is essential.	Many Web sites ask you to complete surveys or register when you make your first purchase. If you intend to visit the site often, providing the bare minimum (required fields) may make using the sites convenient. If you are unsure of the credibility of a Web site, don't provide any information and stop using the site.
Don't reveal personal information inadvertently.	Your browser can reveal your personal details without your awareness unless you change your browser settings. In the browser's setup, options, or preferences menus, check to see whether your name and e-mail address are visible to the Web sites you visit. If you are not using the e-mail component of your browser, remove your name and e-mail address from the Account Settings for e-mail.
Mind your digital cookies.	For maximum security, you can change your browser's privacy settings to alert you to, or block all, cookies. Your security software may offer additional ways to manage the information Web sites' cookies seek.
Limit the personal information you post on the Web or share with others who may post it.	Avoid posting your home address, telephone number, e-mail address, or other personal data on any Web site that can be publicly accessed if you don't want others to gain access to it. For job seekers, a limited amount of contact information is required, such as a telephone number or e-mail address. However, there are few instances when other personal identifiers, such as those listed in Figure 2-1, are necessary.
Remain cognizant of Web security issues.	Never submit a Social Security number, a credit card number, or other financial data over a connection that is not secure. Use encryption if you must provide sensitive information. Never provide your username and password to anyone. With the proliferation of spam and phishing scams online, being vigilant about the types of financial information you reveal can minimize your risk.
Keep your primary e-mail address clean.	Consider setting up separate e-mail addresses to keep communications for your professional and personal lives separate. There are many free e-mail account providers available that make this easy to do. Use the free e-mail account for personal correspondence. If this account becomes over-run with spam or junk messages, you can simply discontinue its use and create a new one.
Read privacy policies and review security seals on Web sites.	Get in the habit of reviewing the privacy policy of the Web sites you visit frequently, especially one where you are asked to provide personal information. Check to see if the Web site backs up its privacy policy with a seal program such as TRUSTe or BBB*OnLine*, which provide a base-line of privacy standards.

Cyberstalking

Corporate recruiters, friends, family, and professional acquaintances are not the only people interested in what you post online. Individuals with less innocent intentions can use the same information sources to commit **cyberstalking**. Cyberstalking refers to the use of the Internet, e-mail, or electronic communications devices to harass another person. Women remain the most likely targets of cyberstalkers, although men and children have also been targets.

In one high-profile case in New Hampshire, a 21-year-old man murdered a 20-year-old woman and then killed himself. For days, the police did not know the motive behind the crime. However, upon confiscating his computer, they discovered he had created two Web sites on which he expressed his loneliness and alternating love and hatred for the woman, who was a former classmate. His online journals revealed how the man had paid Internet search agencies to find the woman's Social Security number and place of employment.

Where do cyberstalkers find their victims? Online gathering places such as social networks, chat rooms, bulletin boards, newsgroups, and online auction sites are all sources. With just a mouse click, a cyberstalker can send e-mail messages to the chosen victim and can even set up time-released messages so the harassment can progress over a period of time. In late 2010, 27-year-old Mitchell W. Hill posed as Lexie Hillbrenner, an alumnus Kappa Delta sorority "sister" who contacted numerous sorority women at several colleges in Alabama, Florida, Georgia, Louisiana, and Tennessee through Facebook. Under the guise of helping to groom them for leadership positions, the stalker started by saying the contact was a normal part of sisterhood, but that they shouldn't tell anyone about their online exchanges. In subsequent chats, Hill raised the stakes by asking the women increasingly personal questions and to send inappropriate photos, and threatened to have them kicked out of the sorority if they didn't comply.

Since cyberstalkers can harass their victims from literally anywhere, it is difficult for law enforcement to identify, locate, and arrest the offenders. Hill lived in Key West but his victims were at prestigious universities across the Southeast. As of this writing, he was charged with two counts of extortion and 12 counts of video voyeurism. All 50 states and the District of Columbia have enacted laws that explicitly cover cyberstalking, and a federal anti-stalking law makes it a crime to transmit any communication containing a threat to injure another person, whether sent via telephone, e-mail, pager, or the Internet. Figure 2-5 contains some tips to help minimize your risk of becoming a cyberstalking victim and what to do if you're being stalked.

Figure 2-5	**How to prevent cyberstalking and what to do if you are cyberstalked**

Tips to prevent cyberstalking

1. Don't share personal information in public spaces anywhere online, nor give it to strangers, including via e-mail, social networks, or chat rooms.

2. Don't use your real name or nickname as a screen name or user ID. Pick one that is gender- and age-neutral, and avoid posting any personal information as part of any online profile.

3. Be cautious about meeting online acquaintances in person. If you choose to do so, meet in a public place and take along a friend.

4. Check the acceptable use policy for your Internet service provider to determine how it handles cyberstalking and complaints. If it fails to provide a timely and adequate response to your complaints, switch providers.

5. If you encounter an online situation that becomes uncomfortable or hostile, log off and go elsewhere online. Contact law enforcement if the situation escalates and you feel threatened in any way.

If you are being cyberstalked...

1. If you receive unwanted contact, make it clear to that person you do not want him or her to contact you again.

2. Save all communications as evidence. Do not edit or alter the contents. Keep a file with a list of all contacts you make with law enforcement and Internet system administrators as you deal with the problem.

3. Unless the communications are needed to help law enforcement catch the harasser, set up a filter to block all unwanted messages.

4. If communications persist after you have asked the person to stop contacting you, inform the harasser's Internet service provider (indicated by the domain name after the @ sign). Most providers have written policies and contacts for reporting complaints.

5. Contact your local police department and inform it of the situation in as much detail as possible. Provide any documentation you have collected to help the police understand the situation.

After reading this section, how would you rate your risk of being cyberstalked? What steps might you take to reduce this risk?

_____

_____

_____

_____

Privacy in the Workplace

Once you start a new job, you shouldn't stop managing your personal privacy. Besides using publicly available sources to learn more about you *before* offering you a position, it's quite likely that your employer will monitor you on the job *after* you start working. In a recent survey conducted by the Society for Human Resource Management and Career-Journal.com, results pointed to technology as a great enabler of on-the-job monitoring. Everything from computer and Internet use to cell phone activity and e-mails comes under the scrutiny of employers. Figure 2-6 summarizes some key findings from the survey.

Another survey in 2007 by the American Management Association and the ePolicy Institute found that two-thirds of employers monitor Web surfing to curtail inappropriate surfing. Forty-three percent monitor e-mails, and 21% have fired an employee over e-mail abuse. Nearly 75% of employers use software for the task of monitoring communications and data traffic to and from their employees. Nearly half track keyboard activity (content and keystrokes); 12% monitor blog posts and 10% watch employee use of social networking sites.

| Figure 2-6 | Employee privacy and monitoring survey results |

Percentage of human resources professionals who agree or somewhat agree that their organizations...	have the right to:	frequently or occasionally:
Monitor employee telephone usage	87%	56%
Listen to employee telephone conversations	41%	17%
Monitor cell phone use in the workplace	76%	48%
Monitor camera cell phone use	86%	18%
Track employee computer usage	90%	70%
Monitor employee e-mail use	87%	57%
Read employee e-mails	53%	30%
Examine instant message usage	87%	31%
Track Internet use	91%	72%

Reprinted with permission of the Society for Human Resource Management (www.shrm.org), Alexandria, VA, publisher of *HR Magazine*. © SHRM

There are obvious competitive and proprietary reasons for employers to be concerned about what employees are doing and sharing via technology. But companies also want to protect against hackers, viruses, and other intruders while maintaining a safe working environment. Employees believe employers monitor them to ensure they are productive, not sharing company secrets, and not applying for jobs outside the organization.

It's not just lower-level employees who are monitored, either. In 2007, Starwood CEO Steven Heyer stepped down from his post after the company's board asked him to explain a series of allegedly suggestive e-mail communications between him and a younger female employee. Personal romantic e-mail communications also were at the center of Walmart former Senior Vice President of Marketing Julie Roehm's wrongful termination lawsuit. Initially questioned regarding the acceptance of a gift from the advertising agency that won Walmart's $580 million account (company policy prohibits employees from accepting gifts), evidence of an inappropriate relationship between Roehm and a subordinate later surfaced in e-mails provided by the subordinate's ex-wife. In these and other cases, sophisticated software is the tool used to sift through millions of messages in search of keywords and language.

A vast majority of companies have written policies covering workplace privacy issues. A smart employee will be aware of such policies and monitoring activity to avoid the consequences of potentially damaging use.

Have you ever been monitored at work by your employer? What activities were monitored? How did it affect your behavior, if at all?

_____

_____

_____

_____

Technology Skills—Creating a LinkedIn Account

LinkedIn has grown to become one of the most popular networking sites for professionals in nearly all professions. In order to demonstrate a sincere interest in your professional career, consider establishing a LinkedIn presence while still in college so you can take full advantage of its networking opportunities when the need arises.

TIP

Sign up for a free e-mail account for professional use through Hotmail.com or Gmail.com before creating a LinkedIn account.

To Join LinkedIn:

1. Connect to the Internet.

2. Open a Web browser.

3. In the address box, enter **linkedin.com**. See Figure 2-7.

Figure 2-7 **LinkedIn home page**

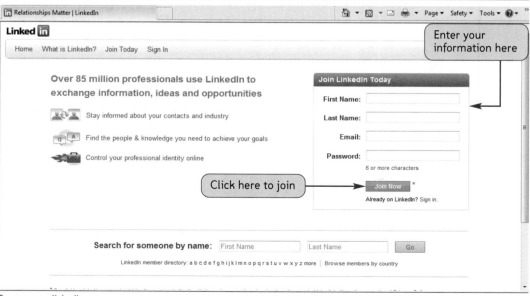

Source: www.linkedin.com

4. Enter your first name, last name, e-mail address, and password in the Join LinkedIn Today box.

5. Click **Join Now**.

6. Complete the requested professional profile information, as shown in Figure 2-8.

| Figure 2-8 | LinkedIn professional profile page |

Add your status and location information here

Click to create your profile

Source: www.linkedin.com

7. If you want LinkedIn to look for people you may know on LinkedIn by searching your e-mail contacts, as shown in Figure 2-9, click the service provider. Otherwise, skip this step.

| Figure 2-9 | Searching for people in LinkedIn |

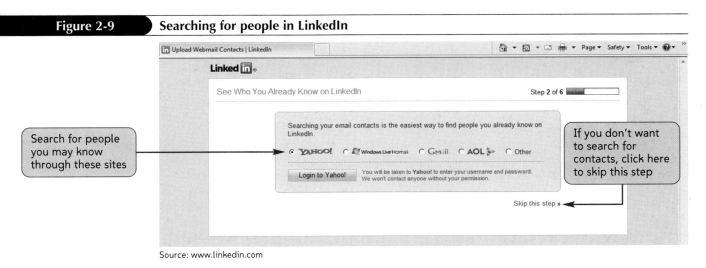

Search for people you may know through these sites

If you don't want to search for contacts, click here to skip this step

Source: www.linkedin.com

TIP

For profile pictures, headshots look more professional than full-body photos.

8. Check your e-mail inbox for a confirmation message prompting you to activate your LinkedIn account. Once activated, you can add a profile photo and additional information about yourself. Remember, this is a professional site—so limit what you post to work-related themes!

Once you've created your LinkedIn account:

▶ **1.** Extend invitations to classmates with whom you want to keep in contact as a working professional.

▶ **2.** If your instructor is a member, ask to join his or her professional network.

▶ **3.** As with other social networks, check back periodically to make sure your information is current and accurately reflects your employment status.

▶ **4.** Open **Word 2010**.

▶ **5.** Launch the **Tech_02.docx** file located in the Project.02 folder included with your Data Files.

▶ **6.** Save the file as **(LastName)_LinkedIn.docx**.

▶ **7.** Answer the questions in the document and save it.

PRACTICE

Personal Identity Theft Protection

Identity theft has been the top consumer fraud complaint lodged with the Federal Trade Commission since 2000, with 21% of complaints in 2009 centering on this crime. So what is identity theft? Basically, it is the theft of a person's identity through stolen identity information. In the most recent survey, the U.S. Department of Justice reports total losses in excess of $17 billion in the United States for nearly 12 million victims. The age group that was targeted the most was ages 16 to 24.

Before completing this assignment, read more on identity theft at the Federal Trade Commission's Web site, ftc.gov/idtheft.

1. Connect to the Internet and launch a Web browser.
2. Enter the URL for the Federal Trade Commission: **ftc.gov/idtheft**. This federal government agency is responsible for handling consumer complaints related to stolen identities, among other things.
3. Open a **blank document** in Word. Prepare a one-page summary of your findings related to the questions listed below.
4. Save your document as **(YourName)_IDTheft.docx**.

QUESTIONS TO ANSWER:

1. What does the FTC mean when it directs consumers to "deter, detect, and defend" against identity theft?

_____
_____
_____
_____
_____
_____
_____
_____

2. What types of fraud can be committed with stolen identity information?

_____
_____
_____
_____
_____
_____
_____

3. How can you protect yourself against identity theft? List at least four practical approaches. If you use a personal social network, such as MySpace or Facebook, include one or two approaches to use in those environments.

_____
_____
_____
_____
_____
_____
_____
_____

4. How might you discover that you have been the victim of identity theft?

_____
_____
_____
_____
_____
_____
_____
_____

5. What steps should you take upon discovering that you are a victim of identity theft? List at least three actions to take.

_____
_____
_____
_____
_____
_____
_____
_____
_____

6. List the top three things you learned from this assignment.

_____
_____
_____
_____
_____
_____
_____
_____

7. The FTC provides information on ways to increase community awareness of identity theft. If directed by your instructor, download the materials provided by the FTC and prepare a presentation that could be given to a local community group, club, or organization.

_____
_____
_____
_____
_____
_____
_____
_____
_____

Cleaning Up Your Online Brand

REVISE

If you haven't given much thought to your online brand, now is the time to do so. Open the **Revise_02.docx** file provided with your Data Files. Follow the actions in each question, and record your results in the space provided in the document. Save the finished document as **(YourName)_OnlineBrand.docx**.

1. Perform a Google and a WebMii search on each of the following and record what the search results reveal:

   a. Your full name (including middle name)

   _____

   _____

   b. Your nicknames

   _____

   _____

   c. Your address (home and school, if different)

   _____

   _____

   d. Your phone number (home and cell)

   _____

   _____

2. Take a critical look at your blog, wiki, Twitter, and social network page postings. Have an adult relative or non-relative you respect critically evaluate the contents of these postings. Based on what he or she tells you, what needs to be removed or made private? Are there any photos, comments, typos, or grammatical errors that might give the wrong impression?

   _____

   _____

   _____

   _____

   _____

   _____

3. Once you've started work in a full-time professional position, what rules or guidelines do you think your employer might have about the use of technology and social networks? How will this affect your usage?

   _____

   _____

   _____

   _____

   _____

   _____

4. Some people don't think it's fair that employers perform background checks and online searches before making job offers, claiming that a person's private life is his or her own business and not the employer's. What's your position on this issue?

   _____

   _____

   _____

   _____

   _____

   _____

CREATE

Online Brand Protection Checklist

Take some time to create a checklist you can use to assess your personal brand protection. Use the **Create_02.docx** file if you'd like to maintain a digital copy of your list.

1. Open **Word 2010**.
2. Open the **Create_02.docx** file provided with your Project.02 Data Files and save the file as **(YourName)_Create_02.docx**.
3. Fill in the date you complete each task on the list; save and then print the document.

Figure 2-10   Online brand protection checklist

Done	Task
	Take some time to visit all the social network sites where you have posted content. Go through each one carefully and remove any content that would give your potential employer the wrong picture of who you are. If nothing else, make your pages private.
	Change any screen names or e-mail addresses that don't portray you in a professional way.
	Sign up for a new, free e-mail account for your personal correspondence.
	Google yourself. Don't stop with just your name—enter your phone numbers, addresses, and any other keywords that might be used to find you. Try other search engines as well, such as Bing, Ask.com, and Yahoo!. Now do the same thing at WebMii. If anything pops up that you don't want others to find, take steps to have the content removed, if possible.
	Try to get cached content removed from Google or other sites. Cached content is old information that doesn't immediately appear when Google returns a hit, but can be accessed by clicking on the link to cached content. Check back every few months because Google often restores archived content from backups—which means that your "removed" cached content will re-appear without your knowledge. Google posts information about how to do this under Help on its Web site.
	Sign up for a Google Alert (google.com/alerts) if you think your name might end up in the news.
	Get a free copy of your credit report at annualcreditreport.com and check it for accuracy. (Note: This is *not* the same site as the fee-based freecreditreport.com.)
	Check your browser's security settings to make sure they are set at the level you are most comfortable with.
	Investigate your current or potential employer's privacy policies with regard to employee monitoring through a Web search, company human resources policies, or the company's intranet resources.

APPLY

Case Study 1

Encore: After the Interviews   As you reflect on Candace Johnson's comments at the start of this project, and what the student candidates did as part of their preparation and follow-up outside the interview setting, take a moment to write a few notes about what you plan to do in the future.

1. Open **Word 2010** and launch the **VideoCritique_Worksheet_02.docx** file located in the Project.02 folder included with your Data Files.
2. Fill in the worksheet with your answers.
3. Save, print, and submit it to your instructor.

QUESTIONS TO ANSWER:

What did Matthew Brady do right? Wrong?

_____

_____

_____

_____

What did Jill Tanner do right? Wrong?

_____

_____

_____

_____

What did Sophie Aguilar do right? Wrong?

_____

_____

_____

_____

What did Tony Bonacci do right? Wrong?

_____

_____

_____

_____

Based upon what you've read, what actions do you need to take to prepare yourself for the interview process?

_____

_____

_____

_____

Case Study 2

APPLY

Create Your Own Branding Web site with Google.com/sites   As noted in this project, a personal Web site that you own and maintain can be a good way to manage your online brand and create a positive Web presence. Google provides a free Web site creation tool at www.google.com/sites. You'll need a Gmail account to get started.

  1. Go to www.google.com/sites. See Figure 2-11.

Figure 2-11 Google sites home page

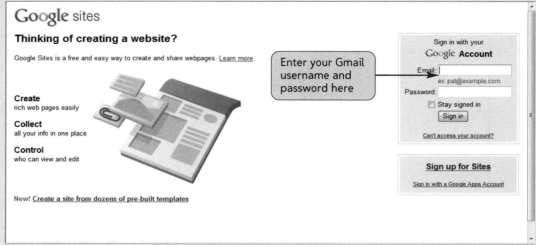

Source: www.google.com

2. Log in with your Gmail username and password. If prompted, answer the onscreen questions.

3. Click Create Site to get started. See Figure 2-12.

Figure 2-12 Creating a Google sites Web site

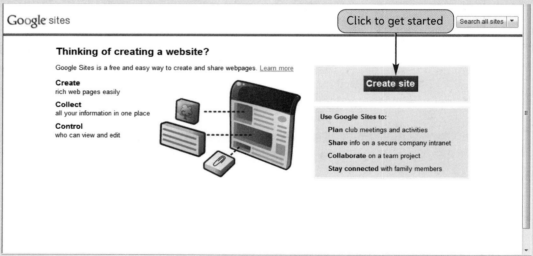

Source: www.google.com

4. Name your site using your full name or something that will identify you as a professional (see Figure 2-13). Make a note of your new URL that can be shared with recruiters, family and friends.

5. Follow the onscreen prompts to populate your new site's contents. Under Choose a Theme, stick with a clean template (not one with plants, clouds or other graphics).

| Figure 2-13 | Choosing a template |

Source: www.google.com

6. Under More Options, select the choices that best fit your planned uses of the site.
7. Your new Web site will appear, ready for you to edit with professional branding content, such as résumé highlights, achievements, projects, and more.
8. If required, send an e-mail link with your URL to your instructor.

Case Study 3

APPLY

Create an Online Brand Survey Using SurveyMonkey   This project has provided a lot of information to help you get ready to enter the workforce. You've had a chance to assess your own personal preparedness, but how do your family and friends stack up? Conduct an informal survey in your residence hall, neighborhood, sports club, or other group to determine your peers' awareness of and concern about their online brands.

First, you'll need to create the survey. One useful Web site for creating online surveys is surveymonkey.com. The site lets you create a free account to design simple surveys, collect responses, and analyze the results. Follow the steps below to create an online brand awareness survey for your family and friends.

1. Connect to the Internet and launch a Web browser.
2. Go to **surveymonkey.com**.
3. Click the link to create a Basic account for free. See Figure 2-14.

| Figure 2-14 | SurveyMonkey home page |

Source: www.google.com

4. Create a username, such as your e-mail address, and password. See Figure 2-15.

| Figure 2-15 | Signing up for a free SurveyMonkey account |

Source: www.surveymonkey.com

5. Enter a survey title, such as **(YourName) Online Brand Survey**. Click the **Create Survey!** button. See Figure 2-16.

| Figure 2-16 | Starting a new survey in SurveyMonkey |

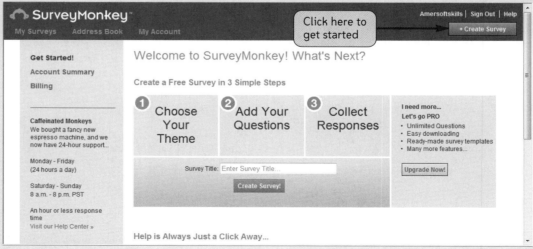

Source: www.surveymonkey.com

6. When the survey template appears, click the + **Add Question** button (see Figure 2-17) and follow the instructions for entering the survey questions below into your online survey. Require a response to each question. You can have up to 10 questions in the free version of the survey.

| Figure 2-17 | Adding questions to a survey |

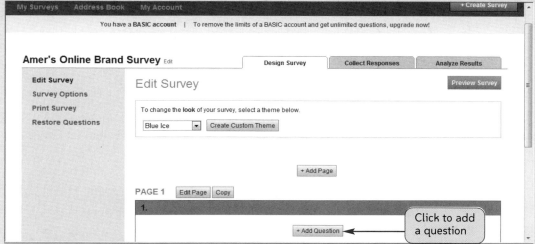

Source: www.surveymonkey.com

a. Did you know that when you apply for a job, companies might do an online search to see what they can find out about you? (Set up this question as multiple choice with only one answer, with "No" as one choice and "Yes" as the second choice. See Figures 2-18 and 2-19. Require a response. See Figure 2-20.)

| Figure 2-18 | Entering survey questions |

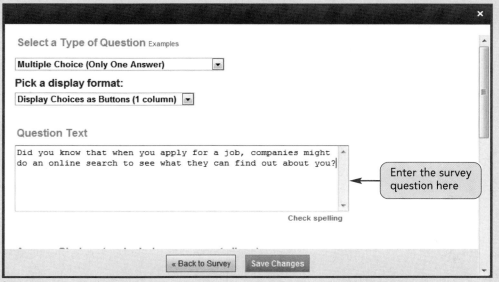

Source: www.surveymonkey.com

Figure 2-19   **Entering answer choices**

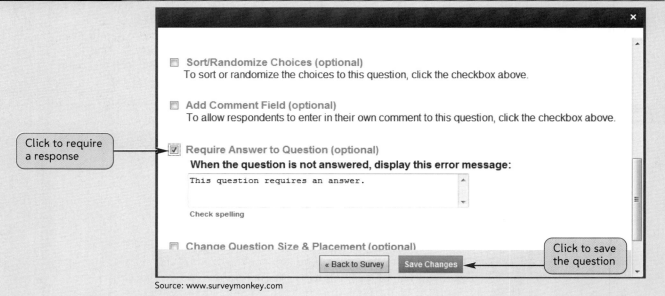

Source: www.surveymonkey.com

Figure 2-20   **Requiring a response to a survey question**

Source: www.surveymonkey.com

b. Do you have personal information posted online that you'd rather your future employer not see? (Set up this question as multiple choice [only one answer], with "No" as the first choice and "Yes" as the second choice.)

c. Have you ever falsified information on a job application or enhanced your qualifications in hopes of getting a job? (Set up this question as multiple choice [only one answer], with "No" as the first choice and "Yes" as the second choice.)

d. Have you ever worked for a company that had rules about social network postings? (Set up this question as multiple choice [only one answer], with "No" as the first choice and "Yes" as the second choice.)

e. How do you feel about employers and other strangers conducting background searches without your explicit permission? (Set up this question as a "Comment/Essay Box" and check the box to require a response. See Figure 2-21.)

Figure 2-21   Selecting a Comment/Essay Box question type

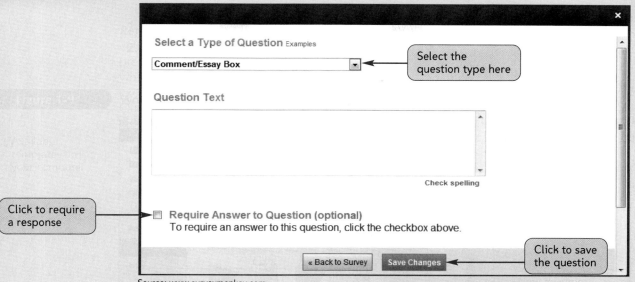

Source: www.surveymonkey.com

> f. What steps have you taken in the past to protect your personal information? (Set up this question as a "Comment/Essay Box" and check the box to require a response.)
>
> g. What plans, if any, do you have to remove questionable content from social networks and search engines? (Set up this question as a "Comment/Essay Box" and check the box to require a response.)

7. Preview your survey. When done, click the **Collect Responses** tab.

8. Click the appropriate choice to select how you want to share your survey. The default choice is to create a link you can cut and paste into an e-mail to send to respondents.

9. On the page with your new survey link, click the **"Change Settings"** tab.

10. Under the "Allow Multiple Responses" question, click **"Yes"**.

11. Under the "Allow Responses to be Edited?" question, click **"No"**.

12. Save your settings and go back to your survey to view its unique URL.

13. Provide the survey URL to family and friends to collect responses. Log out of surveymonkey.com.

14. When you're ready to analyze and report your findings, return to surveymonkey.com, log in, and retrieve your results by clicking on the survey and then clicking on the **"Analyze Results"** tab.

15. Create a Word document that summarizes your results, using one paragraph per survey question. Save your finished document as **(YourName)_BrandSurvey.docx**.

Workplace Communication Skills

Introduction

If you're reading this book, chances are that—like most students—your career preparation skills need some attention. Would it be fair to say your communication abilities could use a little polishing? If so, you're not alone. Solid written and verbal communication skills rank among the top requirements every company recruiter seeks in potential new employees. Personable and otherwise qualified individuals have lost out on great opportunities because they lacked the requisite communication skills. Not fair, you say? So many careers depend on the ability to effectively communicate ideas, processes, and solutions to colleagues, clients, and customers. Therefore, companies simply can't risk making a bad hiring decision.

One area of verbal and written communication that's growing in importance deals with **customer service**. It's one thing to be able to express your ideas and thoughts with colleagues, but every organization has customers or clients who must be communicated with as well. Like first impressions during a job interview, customers make quick judgments about you and your organization based on your communications with them. If your first interactions are positive, you'll win loyalty and repeat business from your customers and recognition from your peers and supervisors. If not, you'll risk not only the loss of business and your job, but also negative word of mouth that can quickly spread and ruin a company's hard-earned reputation.

Another area of communication that many college students need help with is building their **negotiation skills**. Job offers, work assignments, and team project roles all require some degree of negotiation, so applying your writing and speaking skills to these very real and important career situations can affect your success in the future.

STARTING DATA FILES

Project.03

Apply_03.docx
Practice_03.docx
Research_03.docx
VideoCritique_Worksheet_03.docx

Encore Consulting: Video Episode 3

Of the three students in the first interview video from Project 1, Jill Tanner was offered a second interview. After coming in for an office visit to meet the rest of Encore's consultants, both Jill and Encore's team members thought she'd be a good fit for the company and they offered her a job.

Jill accepted the position and has started working, along with another new college graduate, Marcus Jordan. (Tony, from the second video, also accepted a job offer and has been assigned to an out-of-town project.) One of Jill and Marcus' first work assignments has come from Encore's managing partner, Catherine Parker. Catherine has heard that many new college graduates are interested in being entrepreneurial, so she's asked Jill and Marcus to each prepare a one-page overview of how Encore might create an environment to support that interest. Catherine wants to use the briefings as part of the company's quarterly off-site continuing education program for consultants.

After you watch the video episode, analyze and correct the written e-mail and report responses Jill and Marcus sent to Catherine. Use the start file provided (VideoCritique_Worksheet_03.docx) with the Project.03 Data Files. As you complete this project's reading, apply your new knowledge to help Jill and Marcus improve their written communication skills, and in the process, hone your own.

What Your Writing Says About You

> **KEY POINT**
>
> Business writing communicates information needed to take specific action.

Once you enter the workforce, you'll be called upon to use your writing skills every day of your professional life. Nearly two-thirds of salaried employees in professional positions have some writing responsibility. Whether it's a simple e-mail message sent to a group, a memo to provide information on an upcoming event, or a longer project status report or new client proposal, the quality of your writing tells the world how prepared, polished, and confident you are in your ability to effectively communicate.

The study of writing and communication skills in the workplace has received a great deal of attention. In April 2003, the *National Commission on Writing for America's Families, Schools, and Colleges* reported that writing is often the skill most neglected in schools. It further called for the nation to launch a "writing revolution" that incorporates, among other things, more time spent on writing tasks in and out of the classroom. It also suggested that technology could be brought to bear on the development of writing skills so that when students enter the workforce, they'll have confidence and competence.

Half of the corporate recruiters in the study reported that basic communication skills are one of the key items they assess when evaluating job candidates. As noted in Project 1, your first contact with a company is often written—your résumé. To companies, solid writing skills are an indicator of success for higher wage professional work and promotion. If you don't pay attention to writing precision from the start, you may as well tell companies you're not worth hiring because you won't be around long enough to promote. Your writing is really just an extension of who you are and the kind of employee you will be. Why not work on your skills now so you're ready when you enter the workplace?

Common Written Communication Mistakes

> **KEY POINT**
>
> Strong written communication ability is one of the top skills employers desire in employees.

Most written communication errors can be easily avoided yet are often overlooked. Whether you are pressed for time, don't pay attention to detail, or never learned the basics of good writing in the first place, this section should help you turn your writing into works you can be proud to claim as your own.

Mistake #1: Lack of Planning and Focus

Most recipients of business communications are busy and will only read what is important and relevant to them at that point in time. This means you must be succinct and to the point. To do this, you need a plan. Consider the following:

- Think about your audience. Are you writing to colleagues, superiors, or customers? Who will read what you write? What knowledge do they already possess and what attitudes might they have toward your subject?
- What communication channel is best: e-mail, phone call, letter, text message?
- Be clear about why you're writing. Are you writing to inform or do you want action to be taken? Do you hope to change a belief or simply state your position?
- Research your topic. Provide all the necessary information that the reader will need to make a decision or take action. If facts are included, be sure you can substantiate them.
- Don't be afraid to rewrite or revise. If it's an important document, consider having someone else read it so you can determine whether your meaning is clear. At a minimum, read what you have written out loud to be sure the message and impact come across as you intended.

> How often do you take the time to outline your thoughts before writing? What specific items on this list have you neglected that have caused problems in the past?
>
> _____
>
> _____
>
> _____
>
> _____

Mistake #2: Poor Grammar and Spelling

Application software programs such as Microsoft Word eliminate all excuses for not checking your spelling and grammar in written communications. Many e-mail programs even provide the ability to check spelling before sending messages. If yours doesn't, draft your message in a word-processing program first, run a spelling and grammar check, and then cut and paste the text into the body of your e-mail message. Keep in mind that spell-checking doesn't catch every error, so be sure to review your work carefully. If you're not a top-notch speller, this is essential! Also remember that spelling and grammar check tools can't tell whether the words you've chosen are the right ones for your context.

When it comes to writing precision, there are a few basic principles to keep in mind that will make your documents more polished. The first set of principles involves grammar. Figure 3-1 lists some common principles you can apply to your writing.

Figure 3-1	**Grammar tips**

1. Make sure there is subject-verb agreement in your sentences. Pronouns must agree with the word they refer to in person, number, or gender. Examples:
   a. Everyone wanted his or her grades at the end of the exam period.
   b. The faculty is on summer vacation.
   c. The data are conclusive. (*Datum* is the singular form of *data*.)
   d. The alumni of Texas A&M are very loyal to their school. (*Alumni* is the plural form of *alumnus*.)

2. Exercise proper verb tense throughout your sentences, paragraphs, and documents. Proper verb tense examples include:
   a. "Tomorrow I will give blood." Incorrect: "Tomorrow I give blood."
   b. "When the client applauded at the end of the presentation, we knew we had won the account." Incorrect: "When the client applauded at the end of the presentation, we know we win the account."

3. Apply modifiers correctly by placing them as close as possible to the words they modify. When used incorrectly, the meaning of the sentence becomes unclear. Examples:
   a. Incorrect: "The frenzied crowd was brought under control before too much damage could be done by the security forces."
   b. Better: "The frenzied crowd was brought under control by the security forces before too much damage could be done."

4. Avoid run-on or incomplete sentences. Examples:
   a. Run-on sentence: "The music selection was good however I didn't like the second act and couldn't understand what the performers were saying because the volume was so loud."
   b. Incomplete sentence: "The boys at the beach club."

5. Use adjectives to describe nouns, pronouns, or word groups that act as nouns. Use adverbs (usually ending in –ly) to describe verbs. Examples:
   a. Adjective-noun description: "He has a bad cold."
   b. Adverb-verb description: "He did the job really well." (Not "He did the job real good.")

Which grammar principles give you the most trouble when you write?

_____

_____

_____

_____

The second set of principles involves punctuation. Proper placement of commas, periods, apostrophes, and other marks can make a difference in how your sentences are interpreted. A list of some common rules is shown in Figure 3-2.

Figure 3-2	Common punctuation rules

1. Apostrophes show possession or indicate a contraction. Examples:
   a. Possession ("The group's decision is to promote Gretchen.")
   b. Contraction ("This isn't the way home." Or "It's the best movie of the year!")

   Do not use an apostrophe for:
   Plural nouns (DVDs, CDs)
   Reference to a time period or numbers (the 1980s, "She is in her 20s.")
   Possessive pronouns (yours, ours, hers, its)

2. Colons are used to:
   a. Introduce a list of items or an explanation ("Have your child camper bring the following items: a flashlight, a sleeping bag, insect repellent, and a water bottle." Another example: "Life Stories: A Journal for Life's Reflections and Memories")
   b. In business letter salutations ("Dear Mrs. Robinson:")
   c. Maximize the impact of a word or phrase that follows ("There is only one word to describe the event: magnificent.")

3. Commas indicate a brief pause in a sentence and are used to join or separate sentence parts. According to the APA, use a comma:
   a. Before "and" in a list or series ("Steph, Jorge, and Mustafa drove to the beach.")
   b. To separate a direct quote from the rest of the sentence ("I'm in it to win it," the candidate remarked.)
   c. Between two or more adjectives that describe a noun ("Please bring a new, unused gift for the toy drive.")
   d. To separate an introductory phrase or word ("However, that wasn't all that occurred.")
   e. To separate the complete date from the year (October 12, 2012)
   f. To set off geographic names (Boston, MA)
   g. To separate clauses that wouldn't change the meaning of a sentence if they were left out ("The airport, which is located 30 miles south of town, is conveniently located near the manufacturing plant.")
   h. Between names and titles or degrees (John F. Kennedy, Jr. or Susan Elrod, Ph.D.)
   i. Inside a quotation mark in a sentence ("I'll take another one," replied Juan.)

4. Periods are used in certain abbreviations (J.D., Jr., Mrs.) or to end a sentence. If a sentence ends with an abbreviation that ends in a period, no additional period is needed. When a sentence ends with a quote, the period goes inside the quotation mark.

5. Semicolons join thoughts that are independent but closely related. ("My favorite food is pizza; I eat it at least three times a week.")

Which of the punctuation rules in Figure 3-2 have you broken?

_____

_____

_____

_____

The third set of principles covers capitalization. Capitalization indicates importance. Some important capitalization rules are shown in Figure 3-3.

| Figure 3-3 | Capitalization principles |

Capitalize:

1. Full names of companies and government agencies (Apple, Inc., Internal Revenue Service)
2. Brand names, with the exception of Apple's "i" product line and certain other product or company names (M&M's Peanut Chocolate Candies, iPod MP3 player)
3. First letter in the first word of a sentence
4. The letter "I" ("I went to the concert last night.")
5. Proper nouns, names, titles, academic degrees ("Dr. Yang teaches Accounting 255 on the Internet.")
6. Locations, historical periods (Waimea Canyon, The Ming Dynasty)
7. Acronyms (ASAP, RSVP, GMAC)
8. Compass points or regions that are part of an official name (Northern Arizona University, "I was born in the Northeast.")
9. Titles for books, plays, articles, films, and music (The Bible, The Phantom of the Opera, The Seven Samurai, Take Five)
10. Nouns followed by a number (Gate B24, Area 51)

Which of the rules in Figure 3-3 have you violated in previous written communications?

_____

_____

_____

_____

The last set of principles discusses some of the more commonly misused words in business communications. The words, with their meanings and usage examples, are shown in Figure 3-4.

Figure 3-4	Commonly misused terms

Affect To influence or change	**Effect** To bring about a result
Amount Quantity of something not countable in units	**Number** Quantity that can be counted in units
Appraise Valuation or judgment of worth	**Apprise** To inform
Bad Adjective (to connote sadness, guilt, or ill health)	**Badly** Adverb ("I feel badly" means your sense of touch is impaired)
Between Refers to two items	**Among** Refers to more than two items
Can Refers to ability	**May** Permission or possibility
Complement Make complete	**Compliment** Praise
Continual Repeatedly	**Continuous** Without stopping
Envelop To enclose	**Envelope** A container for documents
Except Excludes	**Accept** To take willingly
Farther Longer physical distance	**Further** Greater extent
Fewer For items that can be counted	**Less** For quantities that can't be counted
Fiscal Relates to financial matters	**Monetary** Relates specifically to money
Good Adjective (good luck) or noun (create goodwill)	**Well** Adverb (going well, feel well) or noun (in a deep well)
Illusion Incorrect perception	**Allusion** Hint or indirect reference
In Indicates location	**Into** Indicates movement
Its Indicates possession	**It's** Contraction of "it" and "is"
Like Similar to	**As, or such as** Actual example of something
Regardless (Not irregardless)	
Semi- Twice each period ("semiannual" means twice a year)	**Bi-** Occurs every other period ("biweekly" means every other week)
Site A particular location, as in "Web site"	**Cite** To give credit as a source
Stationary Lack of movement	**Stationery** A form of writing paper
Than Used for comparison	**Then** Refers to a time period
That Refers to people or things	**Which** Refers to things
There At a particular location	**Their** Possessive form of "they"
	They're Contraction of "they" and "are"
Who Subjective form of the pronoun; used when doing the action	**Whom** Objective form of the pronoun; used when the action is being received
"Ann is the one who the package is addressed to."	"Ann is the one to whom the package is addressed."
Whose Belongs to whom	**Who's** Contraction of "who" and "is"
Your Possessive form of "you"	**You're** Contraction of "you" and "are"

Excerpted from Chapter 4 of *Business Grammar, Style and Usage*, with permission of Aspatore Books, a Thomson Reuters business.

Which of the words in Figure 3-4 have you misused in the past?

_____

_____

_____

_____

Precision in writing is also important in the workplace because digital documents often live a long time. They can be used as legal evidence in a court of law. They're often copied or forwarded to people you don't know or intend to be recipients, and who won't know the circumstances under which you wrote your communication.

Based on your writing experience to date, what grade would you give yourself for spelling and grammar? Are you satisfied with that grade? If not, what will you do in the future to raise it?

_____

_____

_____

_____

Mistake #3: Wrong Tone or Language

When you write informal communications, you may use abbreviated or incomplete sentences and phrases or slang. You may even choose to use profanity to underscore your point to family or friends. However, in the workplace, you must carefully consider the tone of your written communication so you don't unintentionally offend your readers. Using contractions is considered friendly and is usually acceptable, but it is never, ever acceptable to use offensive language.

As for the level of formality, once again, consider your audience. A friendly tone is usually welcome in the workplace, as is a positive one. For example, read the following sentence:

"Our customer service representatives are busy and only available between 9 a.m. and 5 p.m. most days, so don't be surprised if we can't answer your call."

How does it compare to this?:

"Our customer service representatives are ready to take your call between 9 a.m. and 5 p.m. Since our heaviest call volume is between 9 a.m. and 2 p.m., please call after 2 p.m. for faster service."

Here's another example:

"We can't possibly fit this project into the schedule before next month."

Compared to:

"We're willing to work with you to help meet your deadline during this busy time of the year."

Do you see the difference? The second sentence in each group conveys the same information as the first one, yet the tone is much more cooperative and friendly.

Reflect on some recent documents or e-mail messages you have written. What was the tone? Could it have been misconstrued?

_____

_____

_____

_____

Mistake #4: Using Clichés and Obfuscation

You probably have a sense of what the word "cliché" means. It is an expression that has become trite and meaningless as a result of its overuse. How about the word "obfuscation"? It means confusion or intentional ambiguity. When you write, your language should be free of obfuscation, clichés, buzzwords, and jargon that will weaken your message or make it difficult for your reader to understand your meaning. For example, it is better to say that you will "set an achievable goal" as opposed to "proactively prioritize target thresholds." In addition, using a bigger word when a simpler one will do can sound insincere and pompous. For example, "Our team will use the resources provided…" sounds better than "Our team will utilize the wherewithal and capital assets bestowed…" Wouldn't you agree? You will impress your reader more by avoiding these mistakes.

Mistake #5: Inappropriate Use of Active or Passive Voice

Using an active voice when you write conveys energy and action. This is the most common way to write in business since it can be used to motivate or stimulate the reader. Active sentences are shorter and have more life. In active sentences, the subject performs the action. For example, you'd say, "Our company is launching a new product…" instead of "A new product is being launched by our company…" for more impact.

Yet in some situations, the passive voice can be effective. The passive voice is softer, diplomatic, and less aggressive. In this case, the subject receives the action. It's often used in situations involving conflict or tension to avoid being too abrupt or blunt. Here's an example: "Layoffs are being initiated by Ancona, Inc. next week." This is the passive voice. Here's the same sentence in the active voice: "Ancona, Inc. is laying off employees next week." Do you see how this one is more abrupt?

Consider these active versus passive phrases. Which is active and which is passive?

- We paid close attention to…
- Close attention was paid to…
- Preference is being given to…
- Our company gives preference to…
- I used the active voice to write this...
- The active voice was used by me to write this…

Reflect on some of your recent writing. Did you use the active or passive voice? Why was that the best choice in that situation?

_____
_____
_____
_____

Mistake #6: Lack of (Storage) Organization

With so much communication now handled digitally, keeping track of all your files is critical. How many times have you searched for a file on your computer because you didn't properly name it or place it in a folder with related documents? The inability to locate a document or message in a timely manner may cause problems down the road. Known as a **storage hierarchy**, creating folders with meaningful names into which you place all documents related to that topic helps keep your **root directory** (your C: drive) neat and organized.

At a minimum, you should have a folder just for application programs, such as Office 2010. The data and documents related to those programs go into separate folders in your *Documents* folder or a similar folder. The names you give to your folders and files can help keep your work organized. A rule to guide the naming of folders and files is called a **naming convention**. Use plain language for the names so that they make sense to you months from now. For example, you might have a folder under *Documents* for this semester's coursework. The folder might be named "2014 Fall Semester." Then, in that folder you might set up subfolders for each course so you can more efficiently keep track of the Word, Excel, and PowerPoint documents associated with each class. The process of organizing folders in this way is called **nesting**. Your naming convention might be something like lastname_firstinitial_projectkeyword. Using this approach, your résumé and an Excel spreadsheet for your class might be saved as follows:

> *Documents* folder (on your C: drive, for example)
> C:\2014 Fall Semester
>> C:\2014 Fall Semester\CIS 120 Course
>>> C:\2014 Fall Semester\CIS 120 Course\Slater_B_PersonalBudget.xlsx
>>> C:\2014 Fall Semester\CIS 120 Course\Slater_B_resume.docx

In the workplace, you can organize your work folders and files in a similar manner. Often, companies provide network storage for work-related documents that gets backed up on a regular basis. If you're currently employed, your employer may have standards for file organization and file naming. If so, use those standards to simplify the task of storing and retrieving your work. It is important to start practicing good file naming techniques now to keep your work organized. One more note: Try to file as you go so you don't end up with a virtual stack of documents sitting in your root directory.

What if you use **cloud storage**? This type of storage is located online, not on your own computer, so you don't own it and can't control it. The same organization approach works there, also. Just be careful about what you store in the virtual network-based cloud, since your company will have policies about where to store sensitive and confidential materials. If you use cloud storage while in school, the same considerations apply.

Ask your instructor for the file naming conventions and preferred storage methods for your class. Is network storage available? How do you access it?

_____

_____

_____

_____

At home, you can mirror the storage hierarchy used at school or work. You'll have additional folders and files at home for family members and personal documents. When working with dated correspondence, include the date in the file name to make it easier to sort and locate. For example, a letter written to Judie Stepner on August 24, 2014 might be named "08242014_JStepner." Later, when you go to find it, you can narrow your search by looking for the date. Don't forget to perform regular housekeeping by purging old, obsolete, or unneeded files periodically. This simple task will make it easier to retrieve important files later by minimizing the amount of clutter you have to sift through.

For personal files at home, what sort of digital storage hierarchy do you need to establish? What naming conventions are needed for folders and documents? What old files are taking up valuable space and need to be purged?

_____

_____

_____

_____

E-Mail, Text Message, or Telephone: Which Is Best?

Your written communication skills apply not only to memos, summaries, research reports, and proposals. They also carry over to digital communications such as e-mail, text messages, and even telephone use. The same principles described earlier in the chapter for written communications can be applied—although the turnaround time may be much shorter for these digital exchanges. In this case, it makes even more sense to apply a bit of forethought and avoid a hasty, careless response that may create unintended consequences down the road.

E-Mail Etiquette

In today's digital world, many people forgo handwritten correspondence (sometimes referred to as "snail mail") in favor of the speed and convenience of a digital form of communication called electronic mail, or e-mail. In a survey conducted by the UCLA Center for Communication Policy, about 90% of people who use the Internet at work use it to access business e-mail.

Although e-mail is a quick and easy way to send messages, writers shouldn't assume that _anything goes_ with regard to the form, content, and use of electronic communications. In the professional world, what you say, how you say it, and when you respond all carry meaning to the recipient. The informal, abbreviated way you write to friends and family doesn't translate well to the professional realm. In fact, when you send e-mail to people you work with but have never met, they instinctively form impressions and opinions of you based solely upon the quality of your writing. Your friendly, upbeat, and casual attitude when expressed through spelling errors, smiley faces, or inappropriate language can actually backfire to make you look immature, uneducated, or worse. At a minimum, you should consider the following items when creating and sending your messages:

- Who is my recipient? If responding to a message with multiple recipients, do I need to "reply all" or just reply to the original sender?
- How quickly does he or she need a response? (A lag of several days may be unacceptable.)
- Have I fully answered any questions or provided the information requested?
- If asking more than one question, could the use of bullets or numbers make it easier to read and respond?

Figure 3-5 provides a checklist of tips that should be part of your professional e-mail etiquette.

| Figure 3-5 | Professional e-mail etiquette guidelines |

1. DON'T USE ALL CAPS. THIS IS THE EQUIVALENT OF SHOUTING in written form.

2. Refrain from forwarding every joke, cartoon, or touching story you receive. Most people don't have time, especially at work, to deal with them and usually end up deleting them or flagging them as junk mail. This means future legitimate messages from you may be tagged as junk as well. Plus, these messages just take up unnecessary space on the mail server.

3. Use proper salutations, such as "Dear Susan," or "Hello Dr. Elrod," or even just the recipient's first name. More informal greetings, such as "Hey, Drama Queen!," are best saved for personal messages.

4. Include a meaningful subject line. Something like "Question about Project 2" is more descriptive than "Question."

5. Close the message with a simple salutation or your automated signature line. This is especially important when the sender's name is not part of the e-mail address or the system doesn't provide the alias for the recipient.

6. Reply promptly, and keep the message short and to the point. Also avoid the use of excessive punctuation!!!!!!

7. Minimize the use of fancy colors or fonts. Using simple, plain text is fine and reduces the possibility of the recipient's mail server not being able to handle the special formatting.

8. Avoid the use of text messaging language and abbreviations. Spell out "you" (not "u") and "your" (not "ur"), and capitalize "I" (not "i").

9. Only use acronyms if you are sure your recipient knows what they mean.

10. Save emoticons for personal communications. Since e-mail can't easily capture the body language or meaning of the sender, they are sometimes used to convey that element. However, they can appear juvenile in the workplace. Instead, focus on making sure what you write won't be misunderstood based on the language and content you include.

11. Don't use profanity. The English language has plenty of rich and meaningful words to help you express yourself without stooping to use offensive language.

Another important caveat about e-mail communications: They are *not* private. As noted in Project 2, the contents may be stored and viewed by your employer—although few take the time or have the resources to regularly do so. Instead, consider what you write in an e-mail message to be more like a postcard. Contents can be viewed by every digital "hand" it passes through until it reaches the recipient's mailbox on his or her mail server.

> Which of the tips from Figure 3-5 apply to your correspondence? For example, are you guilty of typing in ALL CAPS—the equivalent of shouting—or sending along every joke that comes your way?
>
> _____
> _____
> _____
> _____

Finally, respond to all e-mail communications within a reasonable timeframe—within hours or by the end of the day is best. This way, the sender knows you've received the message and you respect what he or she has taken the time to send. Even if you need more time to gather information or check on his or her request with a supervisor, a simple acknowledgement goes a long way toward letting the sender know you are engaged. It also will allow you to avoid the inevitable follow-up call or in-person query: "Did you get my message?" With the growing use of smartphones equipped with e-mail and messaging capabilities, expectations for timely responses may be even shorter in some situations.

Also, remember that e-mail messages are easy to forward—and that, sometimes, recipients "reply all" when they didn't intend to send their comments to the entire mailing list. In addition, be aware that autocorrect may substitute words you didn't intend. Bottom line: Don't say anything in writing that you might regret later.

Telephone Etiquette

The telephone is an indispensable business technology that makes keeping in touch and doing business both efficient and easy. Whether at the office, in transit, or at home, there is no getting around having to use it to keep in touch with colleagues, make meeting arrangements, or broker business deals. Displaying proper telephone etiquette can be yet another way to set yourself apart as a smart and savvy job seeker or employee. Here are some pointers:

1. Answer the phone after two or three rings with a friendly, businesslike greeting. Example: "Hello, Staci Whitman speaking." or "Lancie Render's office, this is Marie."
2. Smile. Callers can tell, even if they can't see you.
3. If answering the phone for a colleague, take the name of the caller before transferring the call or handing it to the recipient. Example: "May I say who is calling? One moment, please. May I place you on hold?" Then don't leave the caller on hold for more than 30 seconds.
4. If you answer the phone for someone else, there is no need to explain why he or she can't answer the phone. Simply say that your colleague is away from his or her desk or the office.
5. Don't talk with food or gum in your mouth.
6. Speak clearly and slowly.
7. Most phones have voice mail. Make sure your message for incoming calls sounds professional. Example: "Hello, you've reached Tanisha Green. I'm not available to take your call. Please leave your name and number after the tone, and I will return your call as soon as possible."
8. If you will be out of the office for an extended period, change your voice mail message to give callers instructions on how best to reach you.
9. When making calls, introduce yourself right away so the recipient knows who's calling. Example: "Hello, this is David Albritton calling. Is Professor Chen available?"
10. When leaving a message, speak slowly. Repeat your name and telephone number so that the recipient has time to write it down without replaying the message.

> Think about how you answer the phone. What signal might your current greeting send to a recruiter, colleague, or senior business associate? How does your greeting need to change to convey that you are a serious business professional?
>
> _____
> _____
> _____
> _____

Cellular Phones

Cell phones present a special challenge for businesspeople today. With over 300 million units shipped by manufacturers every three months, their presence is hard to ignore. Alexander Graham Bell couldn't have imagined the strong emotions that would become attached to the mobile version of his communication invention. Nearly everyone has a pet peeve about cell phones. A study by the Pew Internet & American Life Project confirms that nearly nine in 10 people say they encounter people using cell phones in annoying ways. The worst offense seems to be loud conversations in public places. Can you relate?

No one questions the device's ability to provide individuals with complete freedom to connect and communicate with others from virtually any spot on the globe near a cell tower. It's the *behaviors* exhibited by those users that stimulate the ire of the masses, and this irritation shows no signs of slowing down any time soon. This same study found that more than two-thirds of users say their cell phones would be hard to give up. If this is the case, your knowledge of telephone etiquette must include the guidelines shown in Figure 3-6.

Figure 3-6	Cell phone etiquette

In all situations:

1. Use Caller ID to determine whether to answer.

2. Use voice mail to leave a brief message if the recipient doesn't answer.

3. Don't talk loudly or shout into your phone. If the connection is poor, yelling won't improve the signal strength.

4. Keep calls brief when you are with other people. Doing otherwise implies that the caller is more important than those you are with in person.

5. Practice, by touch, locating the button that will silence your phone in case you forget to turn it off.

6. Maintain a distance of 10 feet or two arms' length from other people when using the phone.

7. Select a non-offensive ring tone. Anything else marks you as juvenile.

8. Consider removing your Bluetooth earpiece when you are not planning to use it. You are plenty cool without it!

9. If you are uncertain, err on the side of courtesy. Set the phone to vibrate or silent mode.

In the office:

1. Set your cell phone to manner mode during meetings. Taking calls during meetings sends the message that the caller is more important than those in the room.

2. If you are expecting an important call that may come during a meeting, inform participants at the start that you may need to step out to take a call.

3. If you are the one making a presentation, don't stop to answer your phone if it does ring.

In restaurants:

1. Turn off your cell phone or set it to vibrate only. If you must take a call, inform your dining partners ahead of time that you may need to step out to take a call. If the call comes, excuse yourself, leave the table, and go outside or to a location that won't annoy other diners. Make the call as brief as possible.

2. With a date or business contact, there are few calls that are more important than the people you are with. If your phone does vibrate, you'll impress your dining partners by silencing the phone, ignoring the call, or looking at the Caller ID and stating you will return the call later.

In transit:

1. If talking on the phone is not prohibited by the transit authority or carrier, speak with a normal volume level. Imagine you are having a conversation with the person next to you; there is no need to shout.

2. Observe the laws of your state when driving. The safest choice is to not use the phone at all.

At social events, theatres, or places of worship:

1. Turn off your cell phone. If you are expecting an important call, such as from the babysitter, set your phone to vibrate only.

2. If a call that you must take comes through, excuse yourself and go to the lobby to take the call.

> What additional cell phone etiquette rules would you add to the ones described in Figure 3-6?
>
> _____
> _____
> _____
> _____

Text, Photo, and Video Messaging

Short message service (SMS) and **media messaging service (MMS)** such as Twitter have become an increasingly common way to communicate using cell phones. In fact, Americans send text messages more often than they make phone calls. With phone plans often including unlimited texting and data options, sending short text, photo, and video messages may be an acceptable alternative when it's not possible to take or make a phone call. Adapt the etiquette rules in Figure 3-6 to your own messaging. Remember, it's better to err on the side of courtesy if you want to set yourself apart. And be sure the content of any message—whether text, tweet, photo, or video—does not compromise your professional image or that of your employer.

> Write down some of the places you've seen people texting or tweeting that you think they shouldn't be. What rules would you add to Figure 3-6, based on your observations?
>
> _____
> _____
> _____
> _____

Everyone Benefits from Good Customer Service

As a child, you may have been taught "*The Golden Rule*: Do unto others as you would have done unto you." Sound familiar? In the realm of customer service, this philosophy goes a long way toward making customer interactions a pleasant experience for all parties involved. **Customer service** is defined as the way employees treat customers. The expectation is that both courtesy and respect will be shown throughout engagements with customers. Good customer service benefits everyone because the goal of the interaction is satisfaction, loyalty, and—for organizations—repeat business. It's much less expensive for a business to keep the customers it already has than to try to constantly attract new ones to keep its revenues flowing. Plus, loyal customers tell their friends and families, which leads to additional business and the potential for new loyal customers down the road.

> Which businesses are you loyal to? Why?
>
> _____
> _____
> _____
> _____

Some people seem to be naturals at interacting with the public. They're outgoing, energetic, and happy, and they have personalities that attract others to them. They're well suited to customer service positions because they're already equipped with the underlying attitudes that customers gravitate toward. Others are not so naturally inclined, so it takes some effort and attention to build good customer service skills. Regardless of your own personality type, it's necessary to nurture and refine strong customer service skills for every level of employee-customer interaction, whether in person, on the phone, or via digital communication such as e-mail or online chat. Why? Just as recruiters quickly judge job candidates on their appearance and writing skills, customers do the same thing with the companies they choose to do business with. As a representative of your organization, you may be the only "face" customers encounter—so your skill in making those instances pleasant is critical.

What constitutes good customer service? There are several key skills you can develop that will make you stand out when you interact with customers in the future.

Skill #1: Positive Attitude and Smile

Approaching customer interactions with a positive attitude and a smile goes a long way toward communicating your interest in helping customers with their needs. A genuine smile, eye contact, and confident body posture (no crossed arms or slouching) signal sincerity. Even if your customer service is offered on the phone, smile and sit or stand up straight, as this will affect your attitude during conversation.

Employees who are new to the job and haven't yet learned all the specifications of products or processes of services can easily overcome those shortcomings with this skill. Many customers will forgive pleasant and helpful novice employees for their lack of knowledge if they can cheerfully and quickly direct customers to someone in the organization who does possess the knowledge or power to help them. Think about it—who would you rather interact with: the store clerk who appears to be knowledgeable about the cell phone you're about to buy but treats you with contempt for interrupting his day, or the newer sales associate who greets you with a smile and seems genuinely interested in helping you but has to consult her manager in order to fully answer your question?

> Have you ever been the new employee who didn't know how to help a customer? How did you respond? If you were in that situation again, what would you do differently?
>
> _____
> _____
> _____
> _____

Skill #2: Listening

Every customer service encounter requires good listening skills. By allowing customers to ask their questions, voice their concerns, or state their positions, you have the opportunity to understand their expectations—what they need—and apply your problem-solving skills toward providing a solution. By quietly listening, you can often determine what the problem, issue, or need might be; and when they've finished speaking, you can pleasantly and politely offer your assistance or resolution.

It's sometimes useful to repeat a customer's request to be sure you understood it, before offering your solution. For example, saying something like "I understand you're having trouble using the online bill payment process. Let me help you walk through the steps." or offering an empathetic remark, such as "I know how you feel. What can I do to make it right?," can point the conversation toward a successful resolution.

> Think about a time when you needed help in a store, on the phone, or online. How well did the organization's employees listen? How did they make you feel, and what was your response?
>
> _____
> _____
> _____
> _____

Skill #3: Others-Centered

When you are "others-centered," the focus of the conversation shifts away from you to what the other person needs. Questions such as "How may I help you?" or replies that are courteous, as in "Yes, Mr. Ravindran, I will take care of it immediately," connote a desire to please and resolve issues the other person is experiencing. Even recognizing that a customer is waiting while you help others, by saying "I'll be with you in a moment," sends a signal that you value the customer and his or her pending interaction with you. When you demonstrate your awareness and willingness to serve others, you show maturity and concern that builds goodwill for both you and your company. Loyalty and repeat business are likely to follow.

When people are recognized as repeat customers, you're placing special value on those individuals. Calling the customer by name, offering a special discount or "preferred customer only" sales notices for repeat business, or other recognition techniques are quite effective in strengthening the relationship. Since most people seek and enjoy the elevated status achieved through loyalty, a simple comment such as "Thanks for returning to our restaurant tonight for dinner. We know you have a choice in where you dine, so we appreciate your loyalty." goes a long way toward building goodwill and showing you are focused on the customer's satisfaction. Many companies use customer relationship management (CRM) software programs that allow them to track recent purchase activity, likes and dislikes, and other personal data such as birthdates so future customer service interactions can be personalized.

> List any loyalty programs you belong to. Why did you join? What benefits have you earned?
>
> _____
> _____
> _____
> _____

Skill #4: Competence and Job Knowledge

How often have you interacted with a store clerk who didn't know how to make change, couldn't or wouldn't provide any product knowledge, or simply treated your inquiries with ambivalence, ignorance, or maybe even as an annoyance? As a customer, you certainly didn't feel valued; and as a result, you may have vowed to take your business elsewhere. Contrast that to the hotel front desk clerk or telephone helpline representative who listened to your needs and offered several ways to assist or resolve the situation.

When you know what you're doing, letting your competence and knowledge show through will instill confidence in customers that you have both the knowledge and authority to take care of their concerns. What if you don't know what to do? Instead of simply giving up and saying you can't help (which leads to greater frustration for the customer), offer to bring your supervisor or a more knowledgeable colleague into the discussion to get it resolved quickly.

> Have you ever interacted with a customer service agent who demonstrated competence? How could you tell? What good customer service qualities or behaviors might you be able to use in the future?
>
> _____
> _____
> _____
> _____

Skill #5: Language, Clarity, and Tone

The language used to respond to questions and the tone of voice employed connote meaning—both positive and negative—to customers. Proper grammar and language usage will signal your respect for the customer. Likewise, avoiding slang or jargon, cynical tones, and snide remarks will keep the customer service exchange cordial and professional. It also helps to speak clearly and enunciate so you can be understood.

Never talk down to a customer—"No other customers have ever had trouble finding the serial number on our product" (translation: you must be stupid because you can't)—or you'll risk alienation and loss of loyalty. Worse, this kind of treatment often leads to customers sharing their bad experience with their friends, which means you've now cost your company their business as well. Use plain language the customer will understand—not technical industry jargon—so your communication is clear. With so many digital ways to instantly share experiences with others—Twitter feeds, blogs, text messages, and more—it's simply not worth risking the viral fallout that can ensue.

> Consider the last customer service interaction you had—at the grocery store, a clothing store, the airport, or a restaurant. Evaluate the salesperson's language, clarity, and tone. Would you consider it to be acceptable? Why or why not? Will you return? Why or why not?
>
> _____
> _____
> _____
> _____

Skill #6: Turning a Negative Experience into a Positive One

Not all customers are happy customers. In fact, all organizations have had the uncomfortable and unpleasant experience of dealing with upset or angry customers. To help diffuse the situation, follow these steps:

Step 1: Listen quietly and patiently to the customer.
Step 2: Try to discern the facts so you can remove emotion from the exchange and address the problem in a rational and logical manner.
Step 3: Remember, most unhappy customers are not personally attacking you, so don't get defensive and let emotion get in the way of resolving the situation.
Step 4: If you are the reason for the customer's displeasure, remain calm. Nothing is gained by firing insults or attacking back.
Step 5: When communicating with customers in person, be sure to watch their body language. If customers are lying in an attempt to get unwarranted concessions, free products, upgrades, or other perks, they'll avoid eye contact with you.
Step 6: If the customer starts to get physical or verbally abusive, touch you, or otherwise encroach on your comfort zone, step back and call in a supervisor or security. Let customers know you can't help them until they calm down.

Step 7: When the customer gives you a chance to respond, immediately acknowledge his or her frustration. Sometimes an unhappy customer just needs to vent and isn't seeking resolution or assistance. Saying "I can understand your frustration. Let me see what I can do." as a response can have the immediate effect of lowering tension, and gives the customer the sense that he or she has been heard and you are willing to assist. Then, check company policy or with a supervisor if you are uncertain about how to handle the issue, and see it through to resolution. A sure way to make the customer even more angry is to say you'll take care of the problem and then do nothing about it.

> Have you ever been part of an uncomfortable or angry customer exchange? What happened, and how did you resolve the situation?
>
> _____
> _____
> _____
> _____

How Negotiation Skills Relate to Workplace Communications

KEY POINT

The goal of negotiation is to reach a voluntary agreement between two parties.

Knowing how to negotiate is a great skill to possess, whether it's used for attaining the starting salary and benefits you desire, working out a solution to a complex problem with colleagues at work, getting a raise, or even getting a hotel room upgrade on a business trip. As a child, you probably developed your negotiation skills when trying to get a raise in your allowance or extend your curfew on school nights, or working with your parents to buy your first car or computer. Successful negotiations can build your self confidence and ability to work with others in the future. So regardless of where your personal negotiation skills stand, this section's pointers will provide you with a way to check and add to what you already know.

> What successful negotiations have you experienced in the past?
>
> _____
> _____
> _____
> _____

Basic Negotiation Skills

You will engage in different types of negotiations during the course of your career. In a "win-win" negotiation, both parties seek to find a solution that works for both sides and leaves everyone feeling as though they "won" at the end of the negotiation process. This type is common in business transactions where both parties will meet again and want to establish, build, or keep a long-term relationship. A second type of negotiation is a "win-lose" situation, where one party is victorious over the other in the process of working out a business deal. Sometimes called "playing hardball," this type of negotiation is usually reserved for occasions when you don't expect to do business with the other party again, as in the purchase of a house or legal settlements. Regardless of the type of negotiation you're engaged in, there are some basic guidelines to follow that will help you do your best to achieve the outcome you desire.

Before you start negotiating, recognize there are three phases to the negotiation process: the **preliminary phase**, the **bargaining phase**, and the **closure phase**. In the preliminary phase, you need to think about *what you want to get out of the negotiation*. How might that compare to what the other party wants? For example, if you're buying a car, your goal might be to get the lowest possible price for the vehicle you want. The dealer, on the other hand, wants to get the highest possible price for the same car. Clearly, your goals don't align, but you both want to close the car purchase deal.

Next, consider *what you bring to the negotiation* that the other party might want. Is it money, time, or other resources such as staff to work on a project? What are you willing to give up in exchange for what you want?

In the bargaining phase, you'll agree to meet and discuss each party's opening offer. Attitude is everything at this point! The place *where you negotiate can affect the process*. For example, if you are negotiating a car purchase in the dealer's sales office, the dealer clearly has the upper hand because you're on his or her turf. Selecting a more neutral location—a third party's conference room or even cyberspace—can minimize the potential advantage location brings.

Depending on the situation, you may offer your position first. For example, stating what you want and then letting the other party respond can get the ball rolling. Other times it's more appropriate to let the other person start to see what he or she offers. As you gain experience with these types of communications, you'll learn *when to go first and when to wait*. You'll also want to be prepared with a *back-up offer or plan*, in case the negotiation doesn't go the way you want.

In a win-win negotiation, the concept of "saving face"—not embarrassing the other party—can go a long way toward reaching an agreement and preserving the relationship for the long term. Intermediaries, such as a real estate agent in a home purchase, an attorney in a lawsuit, or an executive recruiter in a managerial job search, can act as a go-between on your behalf to handle some of the negotiation for you. Remember, in most situations, everything is negotiable, so there's usually a way to work out an agreement that's fair within a range of outcomes. At the end of the negotiation, after all concessions or compromises have been made, you'll come to a *resolution* that is acceptable to everyone.

The final phase—closure—consists of drawing up contracts or agreements, checklists, or other documents that summarize what you agreed upon. There needs to be emotional closure as well, so parties leave with a good feeling about the exchange. Closure then leads to **implementation**, where both parties actually perform what they agreed to do.

If the negotiation breaks down and you can't achieve a mutually agreeable position, what are your alternatives? For instance, if you can't negotiate the right price for the car you want, do you have a second vehicle option in mind? Are you willing to walk away from the negotiation if it's not working for you?

Prior negotiations and your relationship with the other party also affect how you approach the current situation. If you've done business in the past and hope to continue doing so in the future, you may be willing to concede more than desired to preserve the relationship. Often, there will be a chance to negotiate again down the road and gain a concession in your favor the next time.

Finally, think about the balance of power and the consequences of the agreement you'll eventually reach. Does one party hold most of the resources or operate from a position of authority that gives him or her an advantage? At work, your supervisor clearly has some advantage over you when you are negotiating for time off or a new work assignment. Approaching the negotiation with respect and courtesy while being fully prepared with the facts and details of your position will strengthen your positional disadvantage. Figure 3-7 summarizes the basic guidelines presented here.

Figure 3-7	**Negotiation considerations**

Goals	What do you hope to achieve in the negotiation?
Exchange Assets	What do you have to offer, and what do you hope to gain?
Options	What alternatives do you have if the negotiation breaks down?
Relationship	What is your relationship with the other party, and how important is it to preserve it for future exchanges?
Power and Consequences	Who holds the position of power or authority? What consequences might result if the negotiation doesn't go well?

> What was the last negotiation you participated in? Think about how well you prepared, bargained, and closed the deal. How well did you do, and what might you do differently next time?
>
> _____
> _____
> _____
> _____

Salary Negotiation Skills

One of the first major negotiations you'll enter into is the starting salary for your first job after you graduate. According to the Society for Human Resource Management, employees younger than 35 almost never negotiate salary and benefits packages, but employers expect to engage in it as part of the hiring process. In fact, 80% of employers are willing to negotiate, but only 33% of those hired actually engaged in such negotiations! The basic negotiation skills in this chapter still apply here, but there are a few additional steps you'll want to take before you start your negotiation so you don't end up leaving anything on the negotiating table:

Step 1: Research your industry norms as well as local and regional data to see the range of salaries and benefits in your area.
Step 2: Consider the entire package as you negotiate: salary, vacation, medical/dental/sick time benefits, retirement, daycare, on-site concierge, discounts, and other non-financial perks.
Step 3: Start your negotiation above the salary you want to end up earning, so you have room to give. Consider your prior work experience and training. You want to negotiate a package that reflects what you are worth compared to others in the same market.
Step 4: Summarize the skills and background that support your salary/benefits requirements so you can explain why you are worth more than other candidates, if that's the case.
Step 5: Remember to say "Please" and "Thank you" as part of your communications. Respect and courtesy always reflect positively on you in a negotiation.

> As you think about your first post-college job, what elements of your salary and benefits package are important to you? Is anything "non-negotiable?" If so, what are those items? What items would you be willing to negotiate in exchange for those non-negotiable items?
>
> _____
> _____
> _____
> _____

To assist you in negotiating your first salary and benefits package, Figure 3-8 contains some questions you may ask during the negotiation process. Later in your career, an executive recruiter or "headhunter" may assist you in these negotiations. When you ask if the offer is firm, you're confirming that the job is actually being offered at the stated salary. It's fine to ask if the salary is negotiable; but if the company representative says "No," then be prepared to negotiate non-salary benefits such as vacation time, flex-time, stock options, or other perks. If no other benefits can be negotiated, then move on to finding out when the company representative needs an answer. You don't have to answer right away; you should take some time to weigh your options outside the negotiation process. After all, you may have multiple interviews and offers to consider, so leave yourself room for thought and comparison. Simply say, "Thank you for the offer. I'd like to think about it. When would you like an answer?" If you've been offered a better salary and compensation package by another company, it's fine to indicate that you have higher offers, but you don't have to name the other organizations.

Figure 3-8	**Salary negotiation questions**

1. Is this a firm offer for the (name of position) position or is the salary negotiable?
2. In addition to the base salary, what other compensation elements are part of the offer?
3. Is there a probationary or training period with this position?
4. When would you like to have a formal acceptance of this offer?
5. Could I get your offer in writing, please?
6. What signing bonuses are you offering at this time?
7. When does the position start? Is there flexibility in choosing a start date?
8. What is the frequency of performance evaluation? What can I expect in terms of a formal evaluation for salary adjustment or performance bonus at that time?
9. Could you provide a detailed list of financial and non-compensation benefits associated with this position? At what stage do they start to accrue?

Always get your offer in writing, including any information on signing bonuses, additional compensation items (such as vacation time, sick time, retirement plan, health insurance, and stock options), start dates, and other offerings. Asking for a copy of the job description up front is also a good idea to be sure the offer you're given is for the position you're pursuing. If the company isn't willing to commit on paper, then you need to look elsewhere.

As you can see, even the process of a simple salary negotiation—where both parties want a win-win outcome—can be complex. But a bit of research, practice, and willingness to try will help you get better each time you need to negotiate.

Technology Skills – Composing an E-Mail Message in Outlook

E-mail is one of the most prevalent written communication tools in business use today. Knowing how to use e-mail in a professional setting can not only help you effectively communicate with your audience; it can enhance your reputation and set you apart from your peers.

The Technology Skills steps cover these skills:

- Format an e-mail message in Outlook.
- Create a personalized e-mail signature block.

To create a properly formatted e-mail message:

▶ **1.** Open Outlook 2010.

▶ **2.** Click **New** to open a new message window. See Figure 3-9.

Figure 3-9	Microsoft Outlook e-mail inbox

Click New to open a new message window

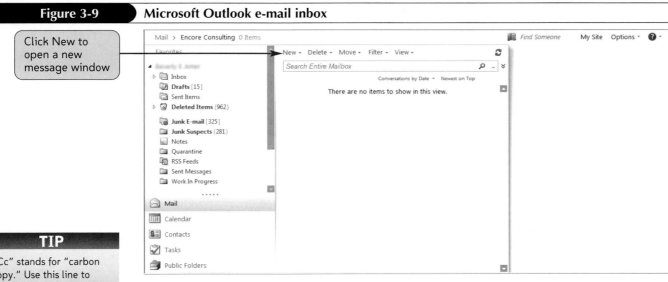

▶ **3.** Enter the **e-mail address** of the recipient in the To... line. See Figure 3-10. If sending the message to more than one person, separate each address with a semicolon (;).

Figure 3-10	Entering addresses for e-mail recipients

Type the recipient's name here

Send a copy to another interested person by typing the address in the Cc... line

Separate e-mail addresses with a semicolon (;) if sending to more than one person

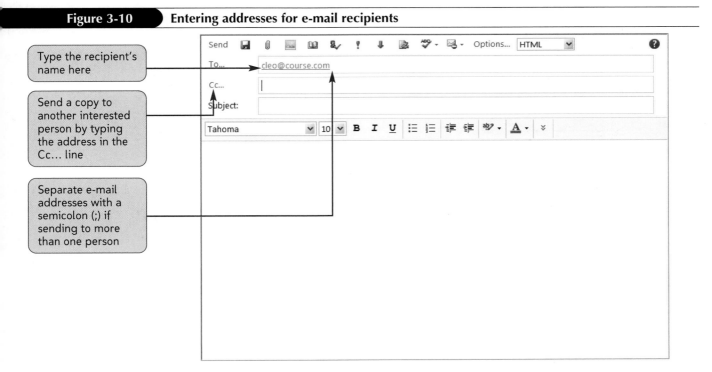

▶ **4.** Enter a **subject** in the Subject line. Meaningful subject lines provide enough information for recipients to get a sense of what the body of the message contains before they open it. See Figure 3-11.

Figure 3-11 Entering a meaningful subject line

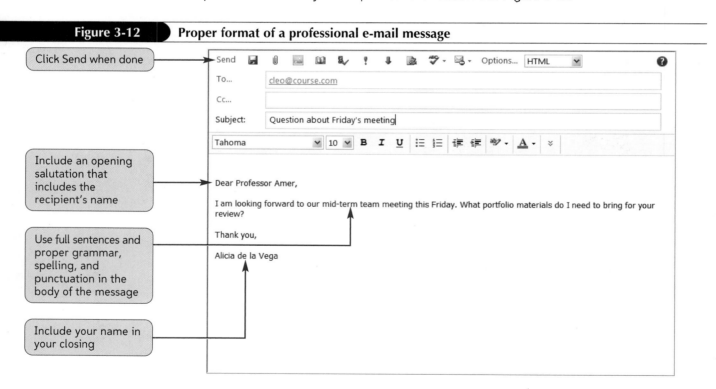

Click the red exclamation point if the message is urgent

Type a meaningful subject line

Send · Draft autosaved at: 9:28 PM
To... cleo@course.com
Cc...
Subject: Question about Friday's meeting
Tahoma 10 B I U

▶ **5.** In the message window, type a **salutation**. Use greetings such as "Dear," "Hello," or "Good morning" before the person's name. See Figure 3-12.

▶ **6.** In the body of the message, use full sentences, proper spelling (no text messaging language or abbreviations), good grammar, and punctuation. See Figure 3-12.

▶ **7.** Finish your message with a **closing** such as "Thank you," "Sincerely," or another phrase that shows your respect for the reader. See Figure 3-12.

Figure 3-12 Proper format of a professional e-mail message

Click Send when done

Include an opening salutation that includes the recipient's name

Use full sentences and proper grammar, spelling, and punctuation in the body of the message

Include your name in your closing

Send Options... HTML
To... cleo@course.com
Cc...
Subject: Question about Friday's meeting
Tahoma 10 B I U

Dear Professor Amer,

I am looking forward to our mid-term team meeting this Friday. What portfolio materials do I need to bring for your review?

Thank you,

Alicia de la Vega

▶ **8.** Click **Send** to send the message. See Figure 3-12.

To create a professional signature block in Outlook:

Professional e-mail correspondence often includes a signature block at the end. Once created, every e-mail you send will automatically contain this information. A signature block usually contains the sender's full name, address, telephone number, e-mail address, and any other contact information that might be of use to a message recipient.

▶ **1.** From the main mailbox in Outlook, click **Options** in the upper-right corner. See Figure 3-13.

Figure 3-13 **Adding an automatic e-mail signature block**

Click Options to add an automatic signature for your messages

▶ **2.** From the drop-down menu, select **See All Options...**

▶ **3.** On the left side, click **Settings**. See Figure 3-14.

Figure 3-14 **Adjusting the e-mail signature block settings**

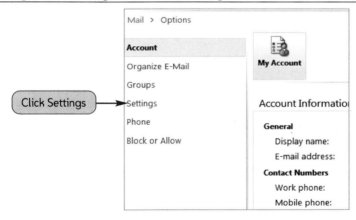

Click Settings

▶ **4.** Type your **Name, Address, phone number**, and **e-mail address** in the e-mail signature box. See Figure 3-15.

TIP

In addition to your contact information, your e-mail signature can include links to your LinkedIn profile, Twitter page, or personal Web page.

Figure 3-15 ▶ **Proper format of a professional e-mail signature block**

▶ **5.** Click **Mail** to exit. When the pop-up box appears, click **Save** to save your new signature line. See Figure 3-16.

Figure 3-16 ▶ **Saving an e-mail signature block**

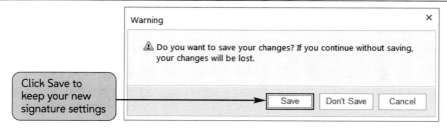

Negotiating a Starting Salary

As you prepare for your first post-college career position, think about how you might communicate in the following scenario. You have just completed a second interview with a company that looks like the best choice. Within a few days, you anticipate getting a phone call or letter extending the offer of employment. Among other things, that communication will include salary and benefits information. As you read in this project, most employers expect some negotiation. So after doing your homework on the acceptable range of salaries and benefits for your region of the country and your experience level, you're prepared.

1. Using the information in this project, write down how you'll respond to the following possible discussion points that could occur as you work out your employment agreement with the company.

2. Use the start file **Practice_03.docx** to record your responses, if needed.

   Company: "We're pleased to offer you the position of entry-level sales associate. The starting salary is $38,500."

   Your response:

   _____

   _____

   _____

   _____

   Company: "The starting salary is firm at $38,500."

   Your response:

   _____

   _____

   _____

   _____

   Company: "I understand your desire to take a few days to think about our offer. What additional information do you need to make your decision?"

   Your response:

   _____

   _____

   _____

   _____

You Write the Report!

Jill and Marcus each attempted to provide Catherine Parker with an overview of workplace entrepreneurship. Can you do a better job of reporting on this recent trend in forward-thinking organizations? Then prepare your own report!

1. In addition to library and online resources, consider interviewing businesspeople in your area to discover what they think about workplace entrepreneurship.

2. Ask your Career Services office which employers have programs for new employees.

3. Conduct an informal survey of your classmates to find out how important entrepreneurship is to them, and whether this type of endeavor is important to their futures and why.

4. If you're already employed, find out whether your company promotes workplace entrepreneurship.

5. After conducting your research, prepare a two- to three-page report that uses standard word processing software features, such as:
   - Headers and footers
   - Citations
   - Footnotes
   - Bibliography
   - Graphics
   - Watermark
   - Word count

Your instructor may require additional word processing features to be used.

A note on plagiarism: Be sure to acknowledge all sources for your information, both through footnotes and in your bibliography. By not giving credit for the information you provide, you demonstrate both unethical behavior and disregard for the original owner's intellectual property. In addition to written policies, schools and professors now have numerous automated tools at their disposal—such as Web sites like turnitin.com—that help them detect such behavior. The consequences can be dire (failure, expulsion) and are simply not worth the risk. If you are unsure about how to properly cite your sources, ask your instructor for guidance.

Using Blogs and Twitter

CREATE

One way to practice your written communication skills is to create a weblog, or blog, or a Twitter following. There are many online service providers that offer the tools and space for all types of written communication—from political commentary and sports talk to personal journals and opinions. While blogs and "tweets"—the 140-character messages sent via Twitter—generally are not considered true journalistic venues, they do offer the masses an easy way to communicate, generate interaction, and be heard in digital form.

In this exercise, you'll create a blog as a way to both express yourself and hone your written communication skills. As an extension of the assignment, consider also creating a Twitter account to promote a cause, provide a platform for opinion, or simply create a following with a purpose you can mention both on your résumé and during interviews with potential employers. After all, tech-savvy companies are using social media to promote themselves and their causes, so why shouldn't you?

1. Choose a topic or theme for your blog or Twitter account. This will become the focus of your writing. Are you passionate about restaurants? Travel? Charity work? What about documenting your educational journey, providing insightful commentary on college life today, or offering soft skills etiquette tips to other college students?

2. Create an account with a blog service provider, such as blogger.com or livejournal.com. As an alternative, open a Twitter account at twitter.com.

3. Follow the guidelines provided by the blogging service to begin creating your entries. Encourage others to read and comment on your entries. With Twitter, follow the site's instructions for getting started. Then, ask your friends and family to start following you so you have an initial audience for your tweets. What should you tweet about? Whatever relates to the topic you chose in Step 1.

4. If directed by your instructor, write a summary of your blogging or Twitter experience for submission and credit.

Case Study 1

APPLY

Encore Consulting: Written Communication at Work   Review Jill and Marcus' e-mail and report materials presented in VideoCritique_ Worksheet_ 03.docx. Using what you've learned in this chapter, analyze, correct, and revise their work. (*Hint:* You may need to completely rewrite some parts!) Next, answer these questions.

1. Read the e-mail messages and reports created by Jill and Marcus.
2. Open **VideoCritique_Worksheet_03.docx** located in the Project.03 Data Files folder.
3. Revise both e-mail messages and reports, and correct the spelling and grammar errors. Note that Word underlines misspelled words with a blue squiggle, and it underlines grammatical errors with a green squiggle. Right-click on **any word underlined with a squiggle** to see a drop-down menu with options for correcting the mistake. You'll have the option to ignore any suggestions if your spelling and grammar are contextually correct.
4. Save your revised document as **(YourName)_VideoCritique_Worksheet_03.docx**.
5. After finishing your edits, answer the following questions:

What did Jill Tanner do right? Wrong?

_____
_____
_____
_____

What did Marcus Jordan do right? Wrong?

_____
_____
_____
_____

Based upon what you've read, what actions do you need to take to improve your own writing skills?

_____
_____
_____
_____

Case Study 2

APPLY

Customer Service Interactions   Practice your customer service response skills by drafting responses to the following customer service scenarios. Use the start file Apply_03.docx to record your responses, if needed.

1. Open **Apply_03.docx** located in the Project.03 Data Files folder.
2. Read each scenario.
3. Write how you would handle the customer service situation presented.
4. Save your completed document with the file name **(YourName)_CustomerService.docx**.

Scenario 1: Retail Store Customer Service Encounter

Alejandro Pena has just walked into your electronics store and is looking for a birthday gift for his nephew who is 14 years old. He's never been in your store before. He knows that computer games are popular with teenagers and wants his nephew to have the latest software as his gift, but he's uncertain about what to buy. You are an experienced gamer and have extensive knowledge about the products in your store. In the space below, write what you would say to Alejandro, what questions you would ask him, and how you would make sure his first encounter with your store is a positive and pleasant experience.

_____

_____

_____

_____

_____

_____

Scenario 2: Insurance Company Call Center

To put yourself through college, you've taken a part-time job working in the call center for a local insurance company. The call center handles all types of customer calls, ranging from inquiries about billing and payments to questions about policies and price comparisons between competitors. Tonight, your first call is from Lucy Begay, who claims she sent in her monthly insurance premium but just received a past-due notice from your company. She is not upset but is concerned that her insurance will be cancelled, and she wants to find out what happened to her payment. You are relatively new to the position but have been trained on how to locate billing information. What do you say to Lucy, and how do you resolve her situation? Write your responses in the space below.

_____

_____

_____

_____

_____

_____

Scenario 3: Angry Customer Demanding a Billing Adjustment

Chris Martin is a regular guest at your hotel in downtown San Francisco, staying for business at least four nights a month. He is a particular businessman—he doesn't like feather pillows, and he refuses rooms near the elevator or ice machine—but he keeps returning. So, as the front desk manager, you assume he is generally satisfied with your hotel's offerings. This morning, however, Mr. Martin has demanded to see you; he called the front desk clerk incompetent after she reviewed his bill with him at check-out. Apparently, mini-bar, room service, and entertainment charges appeared on the bill that Mr. Martin contends are not his, and he wants them removed immediately. He was very vocal in his demands and has gotten the attention of everyone in the lobby. As the front desk manager, what do you say to Mr. Martin, and how do you resolve this situation?

_____

_____

_____

_____

_____

_____

RESEARCH

Case Study 3

Refining Your E-Mail Etiquette   What's your preferred method of communication: cell phone calls or text messaging? The current generation of college students certainly prefers the immediacy of such methods for keeping in touch. E-mail also ranks highly, which bodes well for these students' future success at work. In fact, nearly two-thirds of executives prefer e-mail over other forms of communication, according to a survey by OfficeTeam. Yet there is a big difference between a casual message sent to a friend and a reply to the boss regarding an important client at work. If e-mail use is so prevalent in the workplace, it makes sense to learn the rules early to avoid making mistakes later on.

1. Conduct a Google search for e-mail etiquette. Select the Purdue OWL site (http://owl.english.purdue.edu/owl/resource/636/1/) and one other site to help you gain a better understanding of this important soft skill.
2. Open **Research_03.docx** located in the Project.03 Data Files folder.
3. After completing your research, answer the following questions:

   What advice is provided about sending attachments via e-mail?

   _____

   _____

   _____

   _____

   "Flaming" is a term applied to messages that contain inflammatory, offensive, or insensitive content. Why should the sending of "flame mail" be avoided?

   _____

   _____

   _____

   _____

   Think about e-mail messages you receive. What new etiquette rules should be added to those you've already discovered?

   _____

   _____

   _____

   _____

   What did you learn from this assignment? How will your e-mail communications change in the future?

   _____

   _____

   _____

   _____

4. Save your responses to these questions as **(YourName)_Etiquette.docx**.

Team Dynamics

OBJECTIVES

- Identify workplace team characteristics and the roles you might play
- Practice workplace problem-solving skills
- Learn conflict management techniques
- Develop leadership and supervisory skills

Introduction

In the video episode from Project 1, Encore recruiter Candace Johnson asked Matthew Brady to describe a time he'd been on a team. She wasn't just making conversation. Because most work today is done in teams, companies want to know what kinds of experiences you've had so they can get a sense of how you will do when you join *their* team. If you are like most of your peers, you have spent much of your spare time as a youth engaged in team activities, so such an interview question should be fairly easy to answer. The teams you joined may have ranged from organized sports and musical groups to theatre troupes and debate or chess teams. Your parents knew those activities wouldn't just fill your free time; they also would prepare you for working with others later in life.

It may not have been obvious back then, but your early exposure to teamwork—the joys of setting and achieving common goals, the frustration of motivating slackers—actually was good preparation for what you'll experience in the workplace. As you read through this project's lesson, see how often your own teamwork experience pops into your mind. Those early lessons, plus the information here, just might help you make the perfect contribution when you join your next team.

STARTING DATA FILES

Project.04

Tech_04.docx
Practice_04.docx
Create_04.docx
Research_04.docx
VideoCritique_Worksheet_04.docx

Encore Consulting: Video Episode 4

Encore organizes its consultants into teams that work to support each other as they provide services to their clients. Jill and Marcus have been assigned to the same team and have been working at client sites for the past few weeks. Now the team is meeting to work on its status report for Encore partner Catherine Parker and the rest of the Encore staff. Watch the video episode on team dynamics. You'll meet two experienced senior managers, Erika and David, as well as another team member, Vijay, who may remind you of a former team member in one of your groups. As you complete this project's reading, apply your new knowledge when describing Jill and Marcus' new team and what could be done to increase its chances for success.

Teams in the Workplace

By the time you graduate from college and start working, you likely will have been on more teams than you can count. Everyone on the team probably received a ribbon, trophy, certificate, or something to recognize his or her participation or achievement. In the workplace, the types of teams you'll be on may not necessarily reward their members. But know this: You will work on teams and be expected to do much more than just show up. Unlike school, if you choose not to participate, it won't mean a bad grade. It could result in the loss of a raise, a promotion, or even the job itself.

What Is a Team?

The Web sites of this country's most desirable employers tell potential employees they'll be working on teams from the start. At Google, the Advertising Sales team members "work hard to identify [their] clients' business challenges…" Apple's corporate retail team is "the backbone behind Apple's retail revolution." For KPMG, one of the world's leading professional services organizations, you may be part of a multi-disciplinary team or on a team that is "at the heart of our organization." But what exactly is a team?

The *American Heritage Dictionary* describes a **team** as a "group organized to work together." More than just people thrown together, teams consist of individuals who have skills, talents, and abilities that complement each other and, when joined, produce **synergy**—results greater than those a single individual could achieve. It is this sense of shared mission and responsibility for results that makes a team successful in its efforts to reach organizational goals.

What teams have you been on in the past? What made them successful (or not)?

_____

_____

_____

_____

Types of Teams

In organizations, there are a variety of team types. Some are formal, while others are more informal. Some meet in person; others have members who have never met face-to-face. Depending on the assignment, the type of teams you work on will vary. Knowing a little bit about each one can help make you a more valued member.

Formal Teams

Formal teams are organized within the company as part of its official structure. These teams can be either horizontal or vertical. A **horizontal team** has members from roughly the same level in the organization. When people on a team come from different functional areas of the company—finance, information systems, sales—we often call that team a cross-functional team, a project team, a special-purpose team, or a task force because they usually have a specific problem to solve within a limited timeframe. After the problem is solved, the team disbands.

A **vertical team**, sometimes called a **functional team**, has a manager and subordinate workers from the same department in the company's hierarchy. The manager is in charge and directs the workers as they complete their tasks. This type of team has a much longer life because the work is not single-goal oriented. Functional teams work together to accomplish their everyday tasks. Figure 4-1 shows how horizontal and vertical teams look within an organization's structure.

Figure 4-1	**Different team structures**

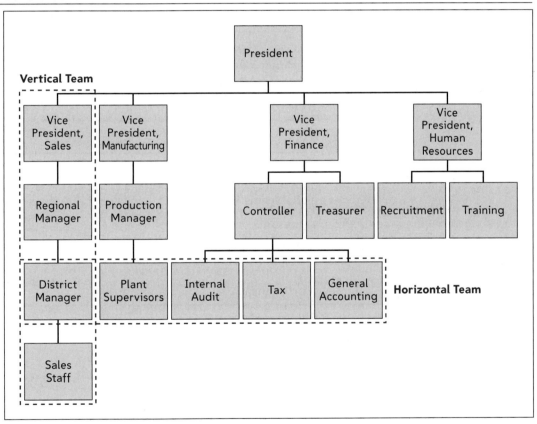

Virtual Teams, Global Teams, and Technology

A virtual team is one whose members rarely, if ever, meet in person to work on team tasks. Instead, technology makes it possible for members to be geographically distant yet work as if everyone was in the same room. Some common examples of technologies used in virtual teamwork include:

- Corporate networks, such as intranets, and cloud storage
- E-mail, voice mail, instant messaging, and text messaging
- File transfer protocol (FTP) Internet sites
- Telephone—both landlines and cellular
- Fax machines

- Teleconferencing, such as audio WebEx® and GoToMeeting® calls, and video
- Groupware and collaboration software tools, such as those found in Office 2010 and Google Docs
- Social networks, blogs, and wikis

Virtual teams often must work rapidly to accomplish tasks, so knowing how best to use these technologies is critical. Some virtual teams also have higher turnover because members will join when their expertise is needed and then leave upon completion of their contribution. The leader may change as well, depending on the stage of work the team is completing.

To make virtual teams function well, leaders must spend extra time ensuring that all members are equipped to work together in a virtual environment. This means building trust early, figuring out how best to communicate, and giving individuals a chance to get to know one another. Because all team members can't gather at a local restaurant after work on Thursdays, for example, using technology to help socialize, share photos, and build a community can make a difference in team productivity. Effectively using digital communication tools, such as e-mail and text messaging, also can increase team member connection and the ability to get work done efficiently.

Have you ever worked on a virtual team? Would you do it again? What techniques and technologies did your team use that made it work well?

_____

_____

_____

_____

When team members are across country borders and span the globe, they often are referred to as **global teams**. Many organizations now have a presence in different countries. These teams are vital for the organization to achieve its goals at both local and international levels. Global team members bring specialized knowledge to the team related to culture, customs, and language. These team members also help other members understand diversity issues related to goal achievement. If you have studied abroad or are multilingual, your experiences and skills may help you add value to the team's work.

If you were asked to be part of a global team, what experiences or skills could you bring? What could you do now (or in the near future) to make yourself more attractive to an employer that has global teams?

_____

_____

_____

_____

Informal Groups

Informal groups sometimes appear in the workplace when the members themselves join forces to solve a problem, work on a task, or simply meet to talk over lunch. Because they are not appointed by management and their duties are not specifically outlined in job descriptions, there is little or no direct accountability or reporting of results to the organization. For example, a group that organizes to clean up the stretch of highway outside the office building won't have management directing its efforts. However, the members may get a nice write-up in the employee newsletter for making their office environs a nicer place to work.

What informal groups have you participated in? Volunteer work? Social committees? How did those groups compare to formal teams you've been assigned to in class or at work?

_____
_____
_____
_____

Characteristics of Teams

Have you ever heard someone say he or she is a "team player"? Members on a team get to know how the others work, so they can make contributions where they'll count most. On a football team, not everyone plays the role of quarterback; the team needs other positions working with the quarterback if touchdowns are to be scored. However, before the first play is ever made, the members bring their skills to the group and spend time learning each other's moves so they can catch the pass, block, or run toward the goal line together. The best teams have members whose background, skills, and abilities complement each other.

Team Diversity and Size

Team diversity comes in a variety of forms. Gender, race, ethnicity, and age are certainly part of it. But diversity also can be expressed in terms of experience, culture, and personality. A team that is too homogenous may lead to average or mundane solutions. A team that is too diverse may require extra effort just to get everyone heading in the same direction. Yet research concludes that a good mix can lead to greater performance and creativity.

What experiences with team diversity have you had? How did diversity affect your team's results? What would you do differently with your next team?

_____
_____
_____
_____

There is no magic number for the size of a team in order for it to function well. However, as a general guideline, a team ranging in size from five to 12 members provides enough diversity for everyone to make a contribution. If there are more than 12 members, subgroups may form, splintering the efforts of the team. Having fewer than five may limit the types of contributions members can make because they may not have the breadth of skills, personalities, or creativity that a diverse team will enjoy.

Think about your last few team experiences. Was the team size too large, too small, or just right? How did this help or hinder your work?

_____
_____
_____
_____

Different Team Roles

Ken Blanchard, leadership expert and author of the classic text, *The One Minute Manager*, has said that "None of us is as smart as all of us." If a team is to be successful for any length of time, members must see the value in both their contribution and what the team gets out of it. This means two important requirements must be met: task performance and social satisfaction. The job of task performance is usually handled by one or more members who are **task specialists**. Task specialists spend a lot of time and effort ensuring that the team achieves its goals. Often, they are the ones to initiate ideas, give opinions, gather information, sort and cull details, and provide the spark that keeps the team on track.

The **socioemotional role** is handled by individuals who strengthen the team's social bonds. This is often done through encouragement, empathy, conflict resolution, compromise, and tension reduction. Have you ever been on a group that had conflict and someone stepped in to tell a joke or soften the blow of criticism? That person held the socioemotional role.

Both of these roles are important for healthy teamwork. It's like the saying, "All work and no play makes Jack a dull boy." Jack as the task specialist needs the complementary skills of the more social Jill to handle the socioemotional side of things for a healthy balance.

What roles have you played on teams in the past? If your team lacked these players, how did it affect the team's ability to do its work?

_____

_____

_____

_____

The task specialist and socioemotional roles are important to teams. However, most teams will have other roles as well, including team leaders, work coordinators, idea people, and critics. These roles are not mutually exclusive. For example, the team leader also might be a task specialist, while the idea person also fills the socioemotional role. As your teamwork commences, these positions will be filled—maybe even by you. On a team, no single role is more or less important than the others. The progress and results the team achieves depend on how well the roles mesh in getting the work done.

Performance Problems

Not every team works smoothly. Sometimes individuals cause problems that interfere with the goals of the team. Others disengage and don't participate at all. This particular problem is called **social loafing**, and is usually the most common human issue teams struggle to overcome. People who are assigned to teams against their will, or who don't have the skill or ability to contribute, may end up "free-riding" on the work of the rest of the team. They get the credit but they didn't do anything to deserve it. Does this sound familiar?

Teams also might suffer from other performance problems, such as:

- Personality conflicts, power struggles, or personal agendas
- Different or incompatible work styles
- Lack of clear goals or direction
- Communication breakdowns

What can you do if a performance problem emerges? If the issue is trivial, you can try to ignore it. When it's important to come to a consensus quickly, try working out a compromise, with each party giving a bit. For situations where the outcome is too important and compromise won't work, a collaboration approach—where both parties bargain and negotiate their way to a consensus that lets both win—could be the best solution. Accommodation, or giving in for the greater good of the group, might work if the problematic parties are both in the wrong and want to resolve the point so the team can move on. Only when a situation is urgent and you need to get your way should you compete against team members to move forward.

> What performance problems have you encountered when working with teams? How did you or the team handle them? How do you think managers in the workplace view teams and members who display those behaviors?
>
> _____
> _____
> _____
> _____

Workplace Problem Solving

KEY POINT

If one team member has a problem, the entire team has a problem.

All businesspeople engage in problem solving in the workplace. Some are better at it than others. But with some practice and by following a few steps, you can learn to quickly diagnose a situation, make a decision, and take the proper action. Most business management books offer a classic model for problem solving:

1. Recognize and define the problem.
2. Determine feasible alternative courses of action.
3. Collect information to evaluate courses of action.
4. Evaluate each alternative's merits and drawbacks.
5. Select an alternative (this is the decision).
6. Implement the decision and monitor the results.

Recognize and Define the Problem

Problems are gaps between an expected or desired state and the existing reality. How many such gaps have you encountered in the past few days? Depending on the magnitude of the problem, you probably started asking questions like the ones listed here to help figure out what happened:

- Why do I think there is a problem—what evidence do I have?
- Where is it occurring?
- When, and how frequently?
- What is causing it to happen?
- Who is involved? (Hold off on placing blame for now!)
- Why is it occurring?

Once you've gathered information, you'll need to analyze it for patterns or trends. Writing everything down can help preserve what you've discovered, in case you need to come back later to re-visit it. You'll also want to talk with people who may be involved, as they're sure to have their own perspective on the situation. Be careful to distinguish the root causes of a problem from the symptoms. Symptoms are just evidence that a problem exists; digging beneath them leads to the discovery of the real issue. How can you tell the difference? Symptoms are the result of something else. For example, is a team member habitually late? You might call that a problem. But why is he or she late? Transportation issues? Work conflicts? Broken alarm clock? Keep asking "why" until you find out.

> Think about a recent "problem" you experienced with work, a roommate, family, or a friend. Ask the questions here. Was that really the problem, or just a symptom of a deeper issue?
>
> _____
> _____
> _____
> _____

Determine Feasible Alternative Courses of Action

Once you've figured out the real problem, brainstorm possible solutions. If needed, write down how you're going to evaluate each one. Don't worry if an idea seems outrageous; those crazy ideas often lead to the best creative solutions. Ask "What if?": What if we had unlimited time or resources? What if we had new skills? What if we could get people to act a certain way? What would we do?

> Consider the problem you listed in the first step. What feasible courses of action did you previously identify? Brainstorm two or three outrageous new solutions and write them here.
>
> _____
> _____
> _____
> _____

Collect Information to Evaluate Courses of Action

Once you've brainstormed, start filling out each idea. A big mistake people make here is that they assume they know everything needed to evaluate options. Instead, talk to whoever had the brilliant ideas and draw out more information. Learn more about the costs, the operational implementation issues, or whatever it takes to fully understand what each potential solution will require.

> Now take each possible solution and expand on it. What do you already know and what else do you need before choosing the best option?
>
> _____
> _____
> _____
> _____

Evaluate Each Alternative's Merits and Drawbacks

Write down the benefits and costs of every option, including both the quantitative (financial) and qualitative components. Use spreadsheet software if it helps organize the details. As you look at the alternatives, start thinking about whether they're affordable, whether there's enough time to try them, whether one is more risky than another, and so on. The best choice is the one that offers the greatest reward for the least risk. It's not a bad idea to have a "Plan B" just in case the first choice doesn't work out.

> What are the pros and cons of each possible solution?
>
> _____
>
> _____
>
> _____
>
> _____

Select an Alternative

Don't get stuck trying to make a choice that fixes every last detail. Solutions rarely are perfect. Instead, consider the effect of the choice you think is most appropriate, given your evaluation of the options. If you've made the best choice under the circumstances, then get to work on how you're going to make it happen.

Implement the Decision and Monitor the Results

The choice is made and your plans are in place. Now it's time to implement the decision. Get in touch with the person or group that's affected by the decision and work through the details of your plan with them. Make sure they understand and buy in to what you're trying to achieve, and follow up periodically to see whether the decision took the course you thought it would or effected the change you were seeking. If so, congratulations! The problem won't resurface. If not, don't worry. Most problems, once solved, often lead to the discovery of others, so you'll start the process over again to work through the new situation and find a reasonable solution.

> Think about a recent problem you identified that had you struggling to find a solution. Was it a work situation or a school team problem? How did you resolve it? If it's still not fixed, work through the problem-solving process to see if any new ideas surface to help you take care of it.
>
> _____
>
> _____
>
> _____
>
> _____

Conflict Management Techniques

KEY POINT

You can only control your behavior, not the actions of others.

Conflict is an inevitable part of the workplace. You're probably already well acquainted with conflict if you quarreled with siblings as a child; clashed with your parents over clothing, friends, or curfews; or have been in groups or teams for school or work. As you read earlier about performance problems in teams, it's apparent that everyone needs to understand why conflicts arise, and more importantly, how to handle them when they do. In some cases, the conflict even can lead to positive results! With the problem-solving approach in this project, you now have a time-proven technique for resolving conflict and getting to those positive results.

Why Conflict Arises

Conflicts arise when there is disagreement or tension between two or more people with different viewpoints, experiences, beliefs, or skill levels. Managers in all organizations will tell you that they respect diversity, which should encompass differing viewpoints, but it's not always the case. Perhaps there is more than one way to accomplish the work tasks your team has been assigned. Whose method is best? Which one will your team use? Or, more often, conflict arises because of communication breakdowns. In the last project, you learned the power of effective personal communication skills. In the workplace, however, not everyone is equally equipped when it comes to e-mail tact, manners, or respect for the opinions and talents of others in a group setting.

Conflict Management Methods

When conflict arises in your next team assignment, awareness of the different approaches you might take can go a long way toward minimizing the distraction and damage it can inflict on the group. There is no single best technique; instead, the details of your particular situation will determine which one to use. Remember to use the problem-solving approach as you work through to a solution.

Approach #1: Withdrawal or Avoidance

This approach may be the best choice when the issue is insignificant or the cost and time involved in resolving it isn't worth the effort. Is a co-worker berating the cashier in the office cafeteria for making incorrect change? What if the co-worker is higher up in the organization than you are? You might risk your career for interfering. Instead, you could offer a kind word to the cashier when it's your turn to pay, and avoid confronting the manager about his or her insensitive behavior.

Approach #2: Accommodation

With accommodation, the goal is to achieve group harmony by smoothing over the differences between two parties. It's sometimes known as the "You win, I lose" approach. You may give in to the other person when it's more important to preserve the relationship than to gain the upper hand or be proven right. When you have a longer-term commitment to a team, this approach can encourage better cooperation. For example, your small office workgroup gathers after work every Friday for a few drinks together. You don't drink and would rather just head home, but you go along anyway (and maybe even offer to be the designated driver) because group unity is important to getting your project completed.

Approach #3: Compromise

This approach is called "Win some, lose some." You will not always get your way; but on occasion, you will. Each party has to give up something in order to meet part way. The result may be dissatisfaction on both sides, because neither one gets everything it wants, but no side loses everything.

Consider this scenario: You're the best technical writer in your company. Independently, two managers from competing divisions have come to you and asked you to work on high-priority corporate projects. Both managers need you to work full-time on their teams for the next few months. What do you do? Both opportunities would be great for increasing your visibility and could lead to a promotion, but you can't do both. How do you choose, or should you? Although many factors might affect how this situation is resolved, compromise may work best because you and your managers will have to work together long after the projects are over. The managers may agree that one of them gets you on his or her team this time, but the other gets first priority next time.

Approach #4: Domination

The domination approach is clearly characterized as "You lose, I win." Often used when one person is in a position of authority or power over another, the will or strength of the authority figure bears down on the subordinate, who has no choice but to give in. This approach works when subordinates must follow their leader, regardless of what they think.

The military is a good example of this. Can you imagine soldiers standing around and debating the pros and cons of the military maneuvers they're about to undertake? Another good example of this is when the actions of one party are unethical or illegal. The offender may think he or she is above the law or that the unethical behavior doesn't really hurt anyone ("I've paid for those office supplies I took home with all the overtime I've worked!"). But the manager may have no choice but to lay down the law to get the subordinate back in line.

Approach #5: Collaboration

When we collaborate, we show mutual respect to each other and agree to actively work together to resolve any issues that arise. This is problem-solving at its best. This approach is the "You win, I win" approach, and is helpful when the teams are ongoing and may be working together for a long time. It may take longer to reach an agreement; but with a commitment to working through any differences for the greater good of the team, a stronger bond and higher achievement may result.

After learning the different techniques, you might decide that you'll always use collaboration because both sides win. But not every situation will permit this. Some conflicts clearly have winners and losers, so being equipped to handle conflicts of all types will help the next time you're faced with one to resolve. Figure 4-2 summarizes the five approaches.

Think of the last team conflict you experienced. Which of the five management approaches was used to resolve it? If you were to do it again, which approach would you use? Why?

_____

_____

_____

_____

| Figure 4-2 | Conflict management approaches |

Approach	Characteristics
Withdrawal or Avoidance	Insignificant or not worth the effort
Accommodation	"You win, I lose"
Compromise	"Win some, lose some"
Domination	"You lose, I win"
Collaboration	"You win, I win"

Steps to Resolving Conflict

If the conflict resolution approach you choose requires that you meet the other party to discuss your differences, the following steps may help you organize your thoughts and keep your discussions moving toward an agreement you can both live with.

1. Meet in private so your discussions are confidential and you minimize the risk of embarrassing each other. Start by acknowledging that you recognize there's a difference of opinion or an issue that needs to be worked out.
2. Focus on deriving a solution, rather than finding fault or placing blame, by focusing on the problem, not the person.
3. Make sure you remain calm.
4. Resist the temptation to get emotional, angry, or retaliatory. Instead, focus on what happened without resorting to name-calling or personal character attacks.

5. Listen to each other's story and try to see his or her side of things. You might discover new facts that change your perspective and can immediately diffuse tension, and vice versa. This is essential in any conflict situation!

6. Accept responsibility for your part of the conflict. If you said or did something to cause the conflict, own up to it and apologize. Sometimes this is all it takes to get the other side to back down.

7. If you can't come to a resolution, get outside help by moving to one of the alternative conflict resolution methods described in the next section.

Which of these steps do you think is the hardest for you to take in conflict situations? Why?

_____

_____

_____

_____

Alternative Methods for Resolving Conflict

In some cases, conflict resolution isn't possible between the two parties involved. Both parties may have agreed at the outset to meet voluntarily to negotiate an agreement, but can't seem to see eye to eye. When this happens in the workplace, you might need to seek help from your organization's human resources professionals, who are trained in conflict resolution techniques such as mediation, arbitration, and adjudication.

Mediation is a voluntary process that involves both parties coming before an impartial third party to help reach a mutually agreeable solution. **Arbitration** uses an independent third party to settle the conflict; but in this case, the arbitrator makes the final determination, which is binding on both parties. **Adjudication** is the option to pursue when the conflict cannot be resolved by other means, because it requires the use of lawsuits, legal professionals, and the court system to drive a decision that both parties must respect. What's important to note here is that both parties give up increasing levels of control the higher up they take their dispute. If it's critical to you to maintain some control over the outcome of the conflict resolution, working it out between the parties or working with a mediator provides greater control than arbitration and adjudication approaches.

Regardless of what happens when you face conflict, consider using the tips in Figure 4-3 to help you and your team members work together better and make the experience a valuable one for everyone.

Which of the tips in Figure 4-3 have you tried before with your teams? What was the result? If any of the tips were ignored, how did it affect the team's productivity?

_____

_____

_____

_____

Figure 4-3	Tips for getting along on teams

- Remember that everyone brings something of value to the team.
- Respect and support each other as you work toward the common goal.
- When criticism or questions arise, try to see the situation from the other person's perspective before taking offense or jumping to conclusions.
- When a team member needs assistance, seek ways to encourage or support him or her so the team's work is not affected.
- Decide early which communication technologies the team will use to keep the flow of information moving smoothly.
- Deal with negative or unproductive attitudes immediately so they don't damage the team's energy and attitude.
- Get outside assistance if team members can't move beyond the obstacle facing them.
- Provide periodic positive encouragement or rewards for contributions.

Leadership Skills for Effective Teamwork

Gaining leadership skills is a key part of becoming an effective supervisor and manager in the workplace. Don't mistake managerial skill for leadership skill, however. Management guru Peter Drucker once said that "Management is doing things right; leadership is doing the right things." John Kotter, an emeritus professor of Harvard Business School and a world-renowned authority on leadership, teaches that the two are related but not the same. When it comes to getting work done, good managers spend time executing plans, watching outcomes, comparing actual results to expected results, and correcting any problems. Good leaders, on the other hand, spend their time motivating and influencing others to work toward the achievement of common goals.

For leaders to motivate subordinates, they must understand what motivates work in the first place. Famous researcher Frederick Herzberg developed a theory called the "motivation-hygiene" theory. He states that "motivation factors," such as opportunity for growth and advancement, accomplishment, recognition, challenging or interesting work, and responsibility, tend to move employees and team members to achievement and greater aspirations. They all relate to the content of the job and are largely intrinsic in nature.

On the other side, Herzberg found that "hygiene factors," such as working conditions, money, relationships, supervision, and company policies and bureaucracy, play more of a role in satisfaction, not motivation. As you can see, the list tends to be extrinsic in nature. When leaders understand the hygiene factors present in their team and workplace environments, both positive and negative, they can address those factors leading to dissatisfaction and better focus on those leading to greater motivation. For example, you may not be able to do much about company policies or salaries; but as a leader, you can certainly recognize a job well done and give high achievers seeking greater challenge more responsibility for complex assignments.

What, then, are the primary characteristics of good leaders? Good leaders have:

- Technical skills and expertise in their area, for which subordinates respect them
- Communication skills, both written and verbal
- Organizational skills to plan and coordinate work activities
- People skills that emphasize collaboration, trust, empathy, and understanding
- Political skills to help navigate the often murky and unwritten rules of the workplace's inner social and power circles

> Think of a time when you were part of a team. Which of these characteristics did your leader exhibit? What did you learn from that leader?
>
> _____
> _____
> _____
> _____

There are many popular tradebooks, expert theories and research, and even entire college courses dedicated to the topic of leadership. Perhaps you've already taken one, or plan to add it to your degree plan in the future. Maybe you even have been in a position of leadership as a captain of a sports team, club president, or shift supervisor at work. Reflect on the list of leader characteristics in Figure 4-4 to determine which skills you already possess, and which skills you might need to develop as you begin your professional career.

Figure 4-4	**Characteristics of good leaders**

- Technical skills
- Communication skills
- Organizational skills
- People skills
- Political skills

> Which of the characteristics of good leaders do you already possess? How and where did you acquire them? Which ones do you need to develop? What's your first step?
>
> _____
> _____
> _____
> _____

Technology Skills—Tracking Changes and Comments in a Shared Document

In today's busy work world, it's difficult for teams to meet regularly in person to accomplish work tasks. More often, team assignments are split between members, with each member making his or her own contribution to the group's output, whether it's a report, presentation, or other combined effort. Working on electronic files, such as report documents, with a team presents a special challenge in tracking the revisions being made as the electronic versions circulate among team members. To make the task of tracking comments and contributions easier, word processing programs, such as Word 2010, contain tools to make digital notations and revisions that can be viewed by team members when they view copies sent via e-mail or posted to a network or cloud storage location.

The Technology Skills steps cover these skills:

- Insert a comment in a Word 2010 document.
- Track changes to a Word 2010 document.
- Delete comments and accept or reject changes to a Word 2010 document.

TIP

To select content in Word, position the insertion point at the start of the content, and hold down the left mouse button while dragging the mouse over the content.

To add comments to a Word 2010 document:

Comments are notes to the reader of a document that are not part of the document itself. They are the equivalent of digital "sticky notes" that you can insert into a document to call attention to a word, sentence, paragraph, or illustration. When the document is shared with others, the comments automatically appear for the reader. Let's try adding a comment to a text excerpt from this project.

▶ **1.** Open Word 2010.

▶ **2.** Launch the **Tech_04.docx** file located in the Project.04 folder included with your Data Files.

▶ **3.** Select the word **books** in the following sentence: "Most business management books offer a classic model for problem solving:".

▶ **4.** Click the **Review** tab.

▶ **5.** In the Comments group, click the **New Comment** button. A new comment box appears, ready to add your text. See Figure 4-5.

TIP

Comments start with the word "Comment" and the registered software owner's ID in brackets, such as "[BA1]." The number after the initials is the comment number.

Figure 4-5	Adding a New Comment

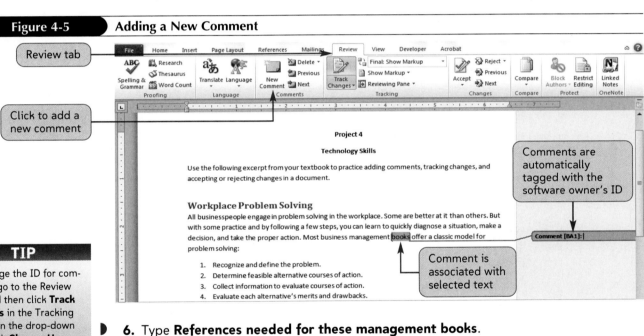

TIP

To change the ID for comments, go to the Review tab, and then click **Track Changes** in the Tracking group. In the drop-down box, click **Change User Name...** and then update the name and initials in the dialog box that appears.

▶ **6.** Type **References needed for these management books**.

▶ **7.** Click off the comment box when you're done.

▶ **8.** Save your document as **(YourName)_Tech_04.docx**.

To track changes in a Word 2010 document:

When making changes to a shared document, it's a good idea to use Word's Track Changes tools to maintain a record of modifications made by individual team members. Here's how:

▶ **1.** Open **(YourName)_Tech_04.docx**, if necessary.

▶ **2.** Click the **Review** tab.

▶ **3.** Under the Tracking group, click **Track Changes**.

▶ **4.** In the drop-down box, click **Track Changes** to turn on the tracking feature. The Track Changes button is now gold to indicate it's selected. See Figure 4-6.

Figure 4-6	Selecting Track Changes

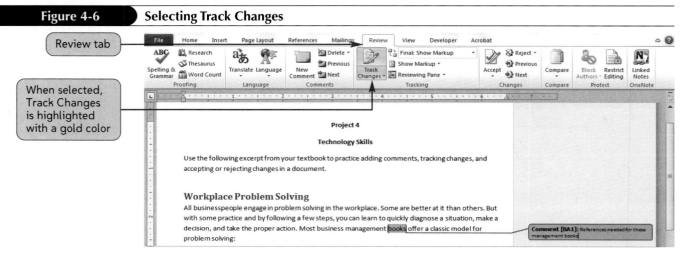

▶ **5.** In your document, delete the "Technology Skills" title by highlighting it and pressing the **Delete** key. The text shows up with a red strike-through.

▶ **6.** Next to the deleted title, type **Problem-Solving Process**. The text shows up with a red underline. See Figure 4-7.

| Figure 4-7 | Deleting text with Track Changes |

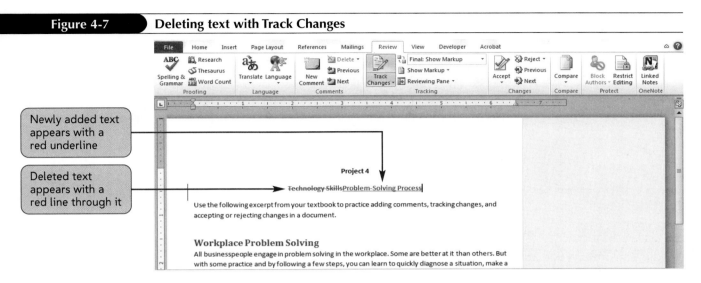

Newly added text appears with a red underline

Deleted text appears with a red line through it

7. Make another change anywhere in the document by deleting or adding text.

8. Save your document.

To delete comments, or to accept or reject changes in a Word 2010 document:

Once you are finished reviewing and editing a document, you need to accept or reject the changes and delete the comments. To delete comments:

1. Open **(YourName)_Tech_04.docx**, if necessary.

2. Click the **Review** tab. In the Comments group, click **Delete**.

3. From the drop-down box, click **Delete All Comments in Document**. Any comments in the document are now deleted.

To accept or reject changes:

1. Click on the "Technology Skills" title, which is red and appears with a red line through it.

2. Click the **Review** tab.

3. In the Changes group, click the **Accept** button. Click **Accept and Move to Next**. The old title is now gone, and the next change, the new title, is selected. See Figure 4-8.

Figure 4-8 | **Accepting changes**

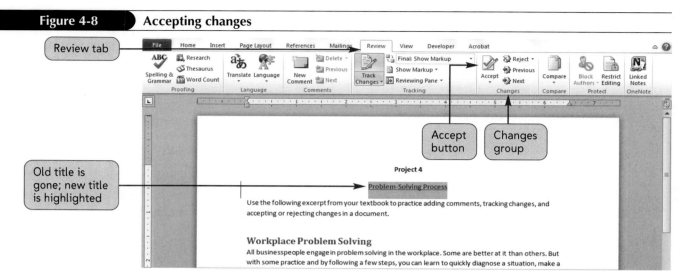

4. Click the **Accept** button again. This time, select **Accept Change** from the drop-down box. The new title is now accepted.

5. Click on the change you made in another area of the document. This time, click the **Reject** button in the Changes group.

6. Click **Reject Change** so the changes are deleted from the document.

7. Save and close your document.

Team Conflict Management

PRACTICE

As you learned in this project, there are different approaches to resolving conflicts in teams. Read the following scenarios and then decide which technique should be used to resolve the conflict. If needed, use the start file, **Practice_04.docx**, located with your Project.04 Data Files to record and submit your answers.

Scenario #1: You're an officer in a service club on campus that is responsible for staging the school's annual scholarship dinner. Everyone in the club has been given his or her work tasks by the group's president. With only one week to go, you've just learned that Sydney, the officer in charge of inviting the school's alumni to the event, forgot to send out the invitations. She's graduating this semester, and this is the last event she's working on. Your club now faces the embarrassing possibility that very few people will show up for the event. Which conflict management method should be used with Sydney, and why?

_____

_____

_____

_____

Scenario #2: You're the newly appointed ethics officer for your company. After creating the course materials for educating employees on the finer points of handling common ethical dilemmas in your business, you've trained all the managers in each division so they can educate their employees. You've just received a phone call from Natalya in sales, who was upset after completing the training with Bill, her manager. She tells you that Bill started the training by stating that he "didn't believe in all this ethics nonsense, but he had to tell us anyway." Which conflict management method should be used with Bill, and why?

_____

_____

_____

_____

Scenario #3: Your employer offers a program that compensates employees up to eight hours per month for performing community service. Because you were an English minor in college, you've chosen to volunteer your time with the reading literacy program one Saturday a month. At the first volunteer training meeting, the program coordinator, Dianne, tells the group that the program she runs is competing this year for a national honor and that she has modified the training materials to now include a strict dress code for volunteers. She doesn't want to be penalized in the eyes of the national program judges because some people weren't dressed professionally. You are well acquainted with how to dress in a business situation and have a number of business casual outfits. Dianne informs the group that she will not permit anyone to wear jeans or t-shirts when representing the program. She also does not want any tattoos or piercings visible. You have a tattoo on your forearm and an eyebrow piercing. Which conflict management method should be used with Dianne, and why?

_____

_____

_____

_____

REVISE

Getting Acquainted with Software Collaboration Tools

As you learned in this project, whether you work on a team is not a question of *if*, but *when*. Most teams you work on will use hardware (cell phones, laptops, etc.) and software applications that make the most sense for accomplishing work and communicating more efficiently. As you learned in the Technology Skills section, features in Microsoft Office make it easier for people to collaborate and share their work with each other. The software enables you to track changes that are made, make comments on what's been written, and much more.

This assignment gives you a chance to learn more about software designed to support collaboration. When your team chooses to use collaboration tools in the future, you'll know what they are and what they can do.

1. Form a group with a few classmates.
2. Have each person choose one of these options:
   a. Microsoft Office 2010
   b. Google Docs
   c. Windows Live SkyDrive
3. Research the collaboration tools that come with the option you chose.
4. Open Word 2010. Write a paragraph about the program. Include a few sentences about what the software does, what its benefits are, and how you envision it being used for teamwork. Save the document as **(YourName)_Collaboration.docx**.
5. Send your written paragraph as an e-mail attachment to one team member for review. Make comments in Word 2010—your team will need to decide how to do this exchange so everyone sends and receives one document. When you get a paragraph from a team member, open the document in Word, turn on **Track Changes**, and make a modification to his or her work by adding a sentence, changing a few words, or deleting a line. Add at least two comments. Refer back to the Technology Skills section of this project, if needed.
6. Save the marked-up paragraph with your initials at the end of the original file name and return it as an attachment to the original sender.
7. When you get your original paragraph back with its comments and changes, open the document. Decide whether to make the suggested changes. For the comments, accept or reject them.
8. Save your revised file as **(YourName)_FinalCollaboration.docx**.

Sharing Documents Online

An alternative to sharing documents via e-mail is to post them to network-based storage in the cloud. Cloud computing tools help groups collaborate, no matter where the individual members are located. One option is to use a Windows Live SkyDrive account. Microsoft offers 25 GB of online storage when you register for a free SkyDrive account. To see how it works, follow these steps:

1. Open a Web browser.
2. Go to **live.com**.
3. Sign up for a free account (or sign in, if you already have an account). See Figure 4-9.

Figure 4-9   **Live.com registration screen**

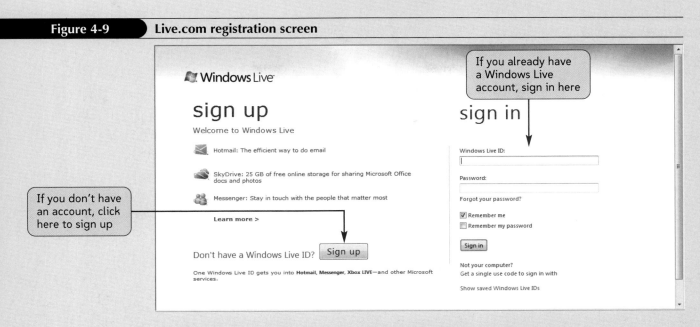

4. Log in to your account with your username and password.
5. Click the **Office link** at the top of the screen. See Figure 4-10. This link takes you to your online cloud storage area. If prompted, accept the terms of agreement.

Figure 4-10   **Uploading files with the Office link**

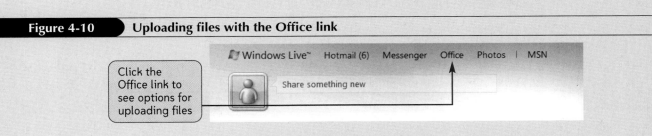

6. Click the **My Documents** folder. See Figure 4-11.

Figure 4-11   **My Documents link in Windows Live**

7. Click **Add Files**. You can add any type of file, including photos.
8. Click **select documents from your computer** to copy a document from your own computer's hard drive to your SkyDrive cloud storage location. See Figure 4-12.

Figure 4-12 Selecting documents from your local computer

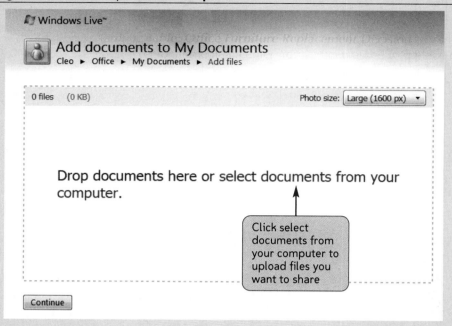

9. Navigate to the drive and folder on your computer where you saved **(YourName)_Collaboration.docx**.
10. Click the file; it's now copied to the My Documents folder on your SkyDrive. See Figure 4-13.
11. To share the file with other Windows Live account holders, click **Share**.

Figure 4-13 Uploading documents to the SkyDrive

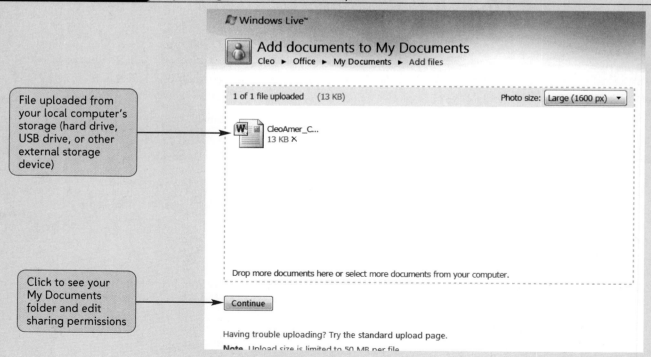

12. Click **Just me**. See Figure 4-14.

Figure 4-14 **Changing the sharing permissions**

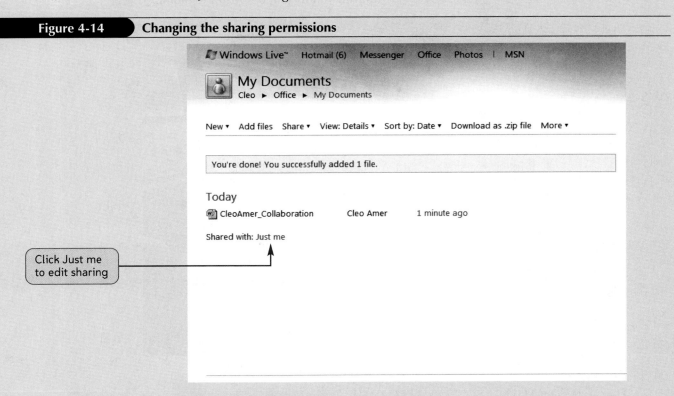

Click Just me
to edit sharing

13. Then, click **Edit Permissions**.
14. Move the slider up to **Friends** under "Who can access this."
15. Change the Friends permissions to **Can add, edit details and delete files**.
    See Figure 4-15.

Figure 4-15 **Changing permissions to Friends**

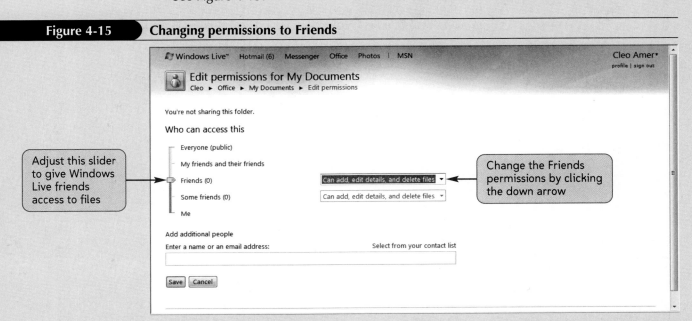

Adjust this slider
to give Windows
Live friends
access to files

Change the Friends
permissions by clicking
the down arrow

16. Click **Save**. Now your Windows Live friends (e.g., classmates who have a live.com account and whose contact information you have entered) can work with your shared folder and its documents. You'll need to let them know the document is available so they can start making changes.

CREATE

Personality Quiz: What Type of Team Member and Leader Are You?

Do you know what type of team member and leader you are? Not everyone is aware of their personality type and leadership qualities. Because this project focuses on teams and leadership, it's worth taking some time to learn yours.

1. Log on to the Web.
2. Go to **personaldna.com** and take the online test to determine your personality type and potential leadership qualities. The test takes about 30 minutes to complete.
3. Print your test results at the end of the online test. Alternatively, your results may be sent via e-mail or posted to a blog.
4. Open the start file **Create_04.docx** and fill in your responses to the questions.
5. Compare your results to those of your team members. Determine who will be your leader, who will maintain the e-mail and phone communications, and so on.
6. Save your completed file as **(YourName)_Personality.docx**.

APPLY

Case Study 1

Encore Consulting: Team Dynamics   Watch the Encore video episode on team dynamics. Then, using the concepts presented in this project, critique Jill, Marcus, and their team.

1. Open Word 2010.
2. Launch the **VideoCritique_Worksheet_04.docx** file located in the Project.04 folder included with your Data Files.
3. Fill in the worksheet with your answers.
4. Save your revised document as **(YourName)_VideoCritique_Worksheet_04.docx**.

QUESTIONS TO ANSWER:

Name	Leadership Skills Exhibited	Team Role(s) Played
Jill		
Vijay		
Erika		
Marcus		
David		

Of the types of teams presented in this section, which type does the team in the video most resemble? Explain your response.

_____

_____

_____

_____

What challenges do you think the team faces?

_____

_____

_____

_____

Which team member is exhibiting the most leadership skills? Why?

_____

_____

_____

_____

Is there any conflict on the team? If so, which approach should be used to resolve it?

_____

_____

_____

_____

If you were a part of this team, what contribution might you make and how would it affect the dynamics of the team?

_____

_____

_____

_____

APPLY

Case Study 2

Using Word and Excel for Decision Making at Encore   With the current quarter's training meeting planned and about to get under way, Catherine Parker wants to start planning the company's big annual meeting. Business has grown and has been profitable, so she's willing to consider taking all consulting staff off-site for the meeting. She has asked all consulting teams to come up with suggestions for where the meeting should be held.

As your team selects locations and gathers information, be sure to consider a few of Catherine's requests:

- One destination researched per team member, with a mix of domestic and international locales
- Resort or urban location with golf, theatre, or local culture to explore as part of a group outing
- At least one restaurant that can accommodate a group of 40
- Upscale lodging
- Reasonable ground and air transportation

Getting started:

1. With a team of several students from class, prepare a proposal for Catherine Parker that provides her with the information she needs to make an informed decision about the best location for the meeting. Your proposal will consist of two parts:
   a. Word 2010 report
      i. Cover page
      ii. Table of Contents
      iii. One-page summary of all locations researched by team members, with your team's recommended choice of destination, transportation, lodging, dining, and activities
      iv. Separate section for each location, with headings and photos that includes the details for the hotel, air and ground transportation, lodging, dining, and activities for the destination
      v. Bibliography of all sources (one bibliography for all destinations)

     b. Excel 2010 workbook

        i. One sheet per location, with the sheet tab labeled with the name of the destination city

2. Your team should prepare an Excel spreadsheet for each location you choose. Each spreadsheet should show the incremental costs associated with travel to and from the destination for 40 employees (transportation, lodging, meals, and leisure activities). For simplicity, assume that the on-site conference costs (meeting rooms and catering) are the same in all locations, so they don't need to be included in your spreadsheet. Your spreadsheet should make it easy for Catherine to compare total costs, so use the same format for all sheets.

3. For international locations, be sure to convert all currency to U.S. dollars (one Web site to use for this is xe.com). The 40 employees will be coming from different cities, as follows:

- Five will originate in London.
- Ten will originate in Phoenix.
- Four will originate in New York City.
- Two will originate in Mexico City.
- Three will originate in Vancouver.
- Six will originate in San Francisco.
- Five will originate in Orlando.
- Five will originate in Tokyo.

4. Ask your instructor to designate a set of dates for the annual meeting.

5. Document your assumptions about which cities the staff will be coming from to help in determining transportation costs. The Internal Revenue Service (IRS) Web site provides information on meal per diem rates and mileage reimbursements as you plan your estimates for meals, and for reimbursements for any consultants driving to the destination instead of flying.

6. Most cities have a Visitors and Convention Bureau that provides useful information for event planning. Major hotel chains provide information about their properties and meeting services. Be sure to include at least one photo of the hotel, and show its location on a map of the city.

7. Save your team's Word document as **(TeamName)_EncoreMeeting.docx**.

8. Save your team's Excel file as **(TeamName)_EncoreMeeting.xlsx**.

Case Study 3

RESEARCH

Team-Building Exercise: Buying a Personal Computer System Here's a small project to help your team learn more about how well you all work together. Your task is to buy a personal computer system for an incoming student at your school. The decision regarding which equipment to buy is to be made as a group, using the research gathered by individual team members. Open the start file, **Research_04.docx**, provided with this project's Data Files. Your budget is $1,200 for everything, including software, printers, storage, and other peripherals.

Part 1 Directions:

1. As a group, decide the student's major. Major: _____

2. Individually, proceed to configure the system you think will be best, using the checklist below.

3. Log on to the Web.

4. Look for Web sites that allow you to purchase computer equipment and systems (e.g., specific brand names or online stores). After completing the checklist, configure a system using the sites of your choice.

5. Type up a summary of your findings, explain why you chose what you did, and be prepared to discuss your choices with your group.

6. As a group, compare your individual results to those of your team members to make a group decision on the best option.

Checklist

1. What does the user need the computer to do?

Class Reports/Presentations		Graphics	
Audio/Video File Management		Online Banking	
Research		Entertainment/Gaming	
Internet/Web		Other: (specify)	

2. Where will the computer be used?

Home		Classroom or Lab	
In Transit (car, hotel, airport, etc.)		Other: (specify)	

3. What types of software must be acquired? (Use the list from #1, above, to guide you here.)

_____

_____

_____

_____

4. What types of hardware are needed? (Be sure to consider all potential uses of the system, and then fill in your selections below.)

Price

1. Computer Brand: _____   _____

    _____   What are the processor specifications?

    _____   How much RAM comes with it?

    _____   What size monitor is included?

    _____   What is the storage capacity of the hard drive?

    _____   What optical drive options are included?

    _____   How many USB ports does the system have?

    _____   Any other special features? _____

2. Printer Brand: _____   _____

3. Software: _____   _____

    _____   _____

    _____   _____

    _____   _____

4. Peripherals: _____   _____

    _____   _____

    _____   _____

    _____   _____

    _____   _____

TOTAL SYSTEM COST (don't go over budget!) $_____

Part 2 Directions:

Team Worksheet

1. Which Web sites did your group use? List the URLs.

   _____

   _____

   _____

   _____

2. Review the findings of each team member and list the best options for the recommended system components here.

Component	Cost	Found by Team Member (name)
Desktop or laptop?		
Processor brand and specifications		
RAM capacity		
Monitor size		
Hard disk drive capacity		
Types of optical disk drives		
Number of USB ports		
Graphics card type		
Other special features (List)		
Printer brand and specifications		
Software		
Other peripherals		
TOTAL SYSTEM COST	$	

3. List the top three things your group learned from this exercise.

   1. _____

   2. _____

   3. _____

Essential Presentation Skills

Introduction

We've all been there—witnessing school presentations given by classmates who don't know what they're talking about, or who drone on without any enthusiasm for their topic. We've watched speakers who don't use any visual aids, use too many, or use the wrong ones to make their point. And, we have seen PowerPoint slide shows that are disorganized or look like the work of a kindergartener. Maybe you're guilty of creating such presentations. Good news! This project will introduce you to a simple approach that you can apply to any presentation to set yourself apart and make a positive and memorable impression on your audience.

STARTING DATA FILES

Project.05

Tech_05.pptx
Revise_05.pptx
Apply_05.xlsx
VideoCritique_Worksheet_05.docx

Encore Consulting: Video Episode 5

At the Encore offices, the quarterly training meeting is being held. Not all of Encore's staff members are present, but most of Jill and Marcus' team has come in for the day. Encore partner Catherine Parker is present and some team members are on speakerphone. Even Vijay made it back from his vacation with surprises for everyone.

Watch the final video episode showing Jill and Marcus giving their presentation for the team at Encore. As you watch, critique their presentation skills using the material from this project and the worksheet questions provided in the start file, **VideoCritique_Worksheet_05.docx**.

Creating and Delivering Effective Presentations

KEY POINT

Thoughtful planning can turn an acceptable presentation into a great one.

The best presentations are planned well in advance of their delivery. The planning process is simple and easy, yet inexperienced presenters often forget some of the steps. No one wants to be seen as an amateur. To prepare for your presentation, you should study the following four-step process.

Step 1: Plan

As you begin preparing for your presentation, consider a few key questions to help you plan what to say. If you can't answer these questions at the start, your presentation will fail to deliver its message or motivate your audience. Conversely, with clear answers to these simple questions, you'll be better able to focus your attention on providing an organized, logical, and meaningful presentation.

- **What is the purpose of your presentation?**
  In other words, what action or response do you want your audience to have? There are only a few types of presentations: persuasive, informative, instructional, motivational, and decision-oriented. If you are making a persuasive sales pitch, you'll want the audience to buy what you're selling. If you are delivering good or bad news (informational), the audience needs to hear the message clearly in order to understand the information you're conveying. An instructional or educational presentation is meant to impart knowledge and provide directions needed to take action. Motivational presentations inspire and stir emotion in the audience. If you want the audience to make a specific decision or take a course of action, then a decision-oriented presentation is the one you'll want to give.

  The key characteristics of each of these types of presentations are listed in Figure 5-1.

Figure 5-1   **Presentation types**

Type	Characteristics	When to use
Persuasive	Short and to the point	Make a sales pitch
	Logical	Sway individual or group opinion
	Fact-based	Convince acceptance of a proposal
	Clear in what you want listener to do	
Informational	Short and to the point	Group needs direction
	Uncomplicated facts	Complex situation needs to be simplified
	Explains when, where or how events need to happen	Delivering good or bad news
Instructional	Explanatory	Novice learners
	Objective-based	Situation needs correcting
	Process demonstration	Practice for skill mastery
	Participatory (hands-on, questions)	
	Outcome is usable skills or knowledge	
Motivational	Inspiring	Develop empathy for situation
	Emotional	Listener is key part of action desired
	Suggests audience be receptive to views	
Decision-Oriented	Logical	Problem needs identification and choices are unclear
	Step-by-step	
	Pros and cons of situation	Action must be taken
	Call to action at the end	Idea presentation

- **Who is your audience?**
  Think about the audience's needs and interests as well as the decisions that will be made as a result of what you say. Timothy Koegel, author of *The Exceptional Presenter*, states that 90% of what you say will be forgotten within 60 minutes. He also states that—believe it or not—the average adult's "undivided attention span" is 15 to 30 seconds. This means what you choose to say to your audience must be relevant to its needs, interests, and decisions or it will be forgotten. Remember to talk *to* your audience, not *at* it. This will help you hold the audience's attention and increase the chances that your remarks will be remembered longer.

- **How much time do you have for the presentation?**
  Some presenters spend too much time on the introduction and end up having to cut their closing remarks short because they run out of time. This diminishes the effectiveness of the entire presentation and leaves a bad last impression on the audience. As you prepare your presentation, consider the amount of time you have so you can pace yourself as you speak.

- **What kind of visual aids do you require?**
  Some presentations are effectively delivered with on-screen visuals. Others require printed support materials because there is too much information to be displayed on the screen, or the presenter wants the audience to have something to take with them to help them remember what was said. By thinking about the finished product, you'll have a better sense of how your message will be viewed and how often it will be seen (via Web or kiosk replay) or reviewed (via print materials the audience keeps for later).

> For your next presentation, consider the following questions: What is the purpose? Who is your audience? How much time do you have? What visual aids are needed?
>
> _____
> _____
> _____
> _____

Step 2: Prepare

Before preparing your presentation, make sure you know your topic. The more you understand your topic, the more relaxed you'll be speaking about it. Your knowledge also will help you answer questions from your audience. This doesn't mean you have to be an expert, but you must be able to correctly pronounce and explain terminology, provide additional information or quantitative data to support your main points, and logically guide your listeners through your presentation from beginning to end.

Once you've done the background research on your topic and feel comfortable that you can explain it to someone who doesn't have your knowledge, it's time to outline what you plan to say. There's a classic presentation maxim that goes like this:

- Tell them what you're going to tell them. (This is your opening.)
- Tell them. (This is your message.)
- Tell them what you just told them. (This is your closing.)

It's a simple but effective way of thinking about how to organize your presentation. As you think about what you want to say, start writing down an outline. Consider your main points first. What logical flow must your points have so your audience will follow you to the conclusion?

Once you've prepared an outline of points in a logical order, think about what you're going to say for each one. Script it out if you have to, and then talk it through. Are you saying too much? If so, start paring your comments back to the essentials. If you keep it short, simple, and focused, your audience stands a better chance of remembering what you said. You need just enough information to help the audience understand your point, but not so much that it overwhelms the audience with details and facts.

Consider the kinds of illustrations, graphics, and audio or video materials you'll need to support what you plan to say. A single image or video clip can go a long way toward making a point and may even help you cut back on the amount of text you need to include.

Once your outline is complete, you can begin putting your presentation into PowerPoint—if that's the medium you think will be most effective at delivering your message. In some instances, you may not be able to use PowerPoint to make your pre-sentation. In those cases, consider whether flip charts, whiteboards, or overhead trans-parencies would be more effective to support what you have to say.

> Think about an upcoming presentation you have to make. Sketch out the main points of your outline here. What visuals do you think should be included?
>
> _____
> _____
> _____
> _____

Step 3: Practice

Presenters who think they can stand up and "wing it" in front of a crowd usually reveal this amateur approach the moment they start speaking—by looking down at their notes, rambling off topic, or turning their back on the audience frequently to read from the slides displayed on the screen. Even the most knowledgeable speakers practice their presentations to ensure they know how the topic flows, what the main points are, how much time to spend on each slide, and where to place the emphasis.

Experienced presenters understand that practice may not make them perfect, but it certainly will make them better. For example, Sir Winston Churchill overcame a severe speech impediment to become one of the 20th century's greatest orators and world leaders. And, as dramatized in the award-winning film, *The King's Speech*, King George VI of Britain worked with a speech therapist to help rise above his speech impediment. Both men spent considerable time crafting and rehearsing their speeches so they would deliver maximum impact on their listeners.

Think about your own experience with practice. If you play an instrument, your music sounds better the more you rehearse, doesn't it? If you're an athlete, your performance in your sport improves as you spend time in training. The same basic principle applies to your presentations.

As you practice, get passionate, speak with authority, and smile. If you aren't excited about your presentation, how do you think your audience will feel? By projecting your voice with energy, passion, and confidence, your audience automatically will pay more attention to you. Smile (if appropriate for your topic, of course), look directly at your audience members, and make eye contact. If your message is getting across, they will instinctively affirm what you're saying by returning your gaze, nodding their heads, or smiling. There's something compelling about a confident speaker whose presence commands attention.

To see how a simple smile affects how you sound, read the paragraph above this box with a serious expression. Then try it again with a smile. Do you hear the difference?

_____

_____

_____

_____

Where you practice isn't that important. You can talk to a mirror, your family, or a group of friends. If you have a video camera, record yourself and then review the video. Sometimes it can be painful to watch video evidence of your performance, but it often reveals the weaknesses you don't want your audience to see and that your friends or family may be unwilling or unable to identify. Whatever you choose to do, the bottom line is this: If you practice, you will improve.

Think about the best presenters you've ever seen. How passionate were they about their topic? What makes you think so? Would their presentation have been as effective if it had been delivered in a slow monotone voice?

_____

_____

_____

_____

> What approaches to practicing do you think you will be comfortable using? If you've used one of these techniques before, what did you learn?
>
> _____
> _____
> _____
> _____
> _____

Step 4: Present

You've planned, prepared, and practiced. The only thing left to do is to present! You know _what_ you're going to say and _how_ you're going to say it. As you make your presentation, relax, smile, and take your time. By taking a few deep breaths at the start, making eye contact with members of your audience, and knowing that you have done the work to get to this point, you should do just fine.

Applying Decision-Making Steps to Presentations

The four-step planning process just described is a time-proven approach. But underlying the steps is an even more fundamental process: decision making. **Decision making** is the process of choosing between alternative courses of action generated from following a problem-solving process. As you learned in the last project, **problem solving** requires gathering, giving, receiving, and processing information from various sources in order to solve a dilemma. Making presentations is an efficient part of the communication process in all organizations because managers, employees, customers, suppliers, and others want to be informed. The steps explained in this next section describe how business decisions are made. But you can adapt them for deciding how to organize your future presentations and what types of information to include.

Step 1: Gather Relevant Information

No matter what type of presentation you're giving, you'll want to have all the relevant information at your disposal. The relevant information might include quantitative financial information such as revenues and expenses, and qualitative factors such as customer opinion surveys or information regarding the economy and legislative action. This information not only will be useful for the decision itself, but can become part of the presentations you'll make to customers, management, employees, and other interested groups to help explain what's happening as it unfolds.

Step 2: Make Predictions

What are your decision choices? After collecting relevant information, use the information to analyze your options and make predictions about different outcomes that could result from one choice or another. In organizations, a variety of decision-making tools exist to help structure decision processes. One popular tool is the **decision table**. These tables use probability estimates to help determine the likelihood of certain events.

For example, let's say your presentation is a decision-oriented overview that involves helping your company's management team choose what expansion plan to use. The first option is to lease a large space to create a "signature brand" store in an upscale mall. The second option is to lease a smaller space in a historic downtown location and create a boutique. In a favorable economy, your company expects the upscale signature brand store to generate a net profit of $200,000. If the economy is not favorable, a net loss of

$180,000 is expected. The small boutique, on the other hand, will generate a net profit of only $100,000 in a favorable economy, but just a $20,000 net loss in an unfavorable economy. Of course, the third option is that you could always do nothing, which results in no income at all. So which option does your organization choose?

Using a decision table, you can set up the quantitative information needed to evaluate the options, as shown in Figure 5-2.

Figure 5-2 **Decision table**

Alternatives	Favorable economy	Unfavorable economy
Open signature brand store	$200,000	–$180,000
Open small boutique	$100,000	–$ 20,000
Do nothing	$0	$0

Decision making always takes place under one of several situations: under certainty, under risk, and under uncertainty. With **decision making under certainty**, you'll know which event will occur. For your decision, you'll choose the one with the highest pay-off. For the retail example, if your company is certain the economy will be favorable, the choice is to open the upscale signature brand store with the expected net profit of $200,000.

With **decision making under risk**, probabilities come into play. For each alternative, a probability is assigned to the expected outcomes, called states of nature, so that pay-offs may be calculated based on perceived frequency of occurrence. For the retail store example, your company may determine that there's a 55% probability of a favorable economy and a 45% probability of an unfavorable one. Decision models for this type of scenario use calculations of the **expected monetary value** (EMV) of each outcome. The EMV is what the average payoff would be if the decision were made repeatedly. The scenario with the highest EMV is the best choice. Figure 5-3 shows your company's retail decision table with probabilities added.

Figure 5-3 **Decision table with probabilities**

	States of nature	
Alternatives	**Favorable economy**	**Unfavorable economy**
Open signature brand store	$200,000	–$180,000
Open small boutique	$100,000	–$ 20,000
Do nothing	$0	$0
Probabilities	.55	.45

EMV (signature brand store): (.55)($200,000)+(.45)(–$180,000) = $29,000

EMV (small boutique store): (.55)($100,000)+(.45)(–$20,000) = $46,000

EMV (doing nothing): (.55)($0)+(.45)($0) = $0

Calculating the EMV for the upscale signature brand store looks like this:

(.55)($200,000)+(.45)(–$180,000) = $29,000

The EMV of opening the small boutique store is:

(.55)($100,000)+(.45)(–$20,000) = $46,000

The EMV of doing nothing is:

(.55)($0)+(.45)($0) = $0

Can you see which choice your company should consider first? It's opening the small boutique store because the EMV is the highest, at $46,000.

Decision making under uncertainty is the greatest challenge because it's not even possible to assign a probability to each scenario. In this case, you rely on three approaches: optimistic, pessimistic, and equally likely outcomes. For the optimistic outcome, your choice is the "best of the best" for each alternative. For the pessimistic outcome, your choice is the "best of the worst" for each outcome. For the equally likely outcome, your choice is the maximum of the average outcome for each alternative because it assumes all outcomes are equally likely to occur. Figure 5-4 shows the calculations for each alternative.

Figure 5-4	Decision table for decision making under uncertainty

Alternatives	States of nature				
	Favorable economy	Unfavorable economy	Maximum in row	Minimum in row	Row average
Open signature brand store	$200,000	–$180,000	$200,000	–$180,000	$10,000
Open small boutique	$100,000	–$ 20,000	$100,000	–$ 20,000	$40,000
Do nothing	$0	$0	$0	$0	$0

Optimistic outcome   Pessimistic outcome   Equally likely outcomes

For the optimistic outcome, the maximum—"best of the best"—is $200,000. So if your company was optimistic, it would choose to open the signature brand store. If your company was pessimistic, it would choose to do nothing because the outcome is $0—the "best of the worst." Can you see which alternative to choose if all outcomes are equally likely? It's opening the small boutique because it has the highest row average at $40,000.

Sometimes a decision needs to be made quickly yet still requires some analysis. In this case, a **weighting and ranking table** can be used to capture the relative importance of variables related to decision alternatives. It is especially valuable when quantifying the variables is a challenge or when the variables are qualitative in nature.

Let's consider a decision you might face at work. You've been asked to decide where to hold an internal company meeting. You could reserve a large conference room for a day in your organization's own offices, or you could go off-site. The off-site locations could be across town or out of state. Where do you start? List all the factors that will play a role in your decision, such as the ease of getting everyone to the location, presentation technology available for your use at the location, cost, impact on work activities, and employee reaction.

Next, you'll create your weighting and ranking table, as shown in Figure 5-5.

Figure 5-5	Weighting and ranking table

Factors	Ease of getting team to location		Presentation technology available at location		Cost (meals, transportation, lodging)		Impact on work activities		Employee reaction		Total points
Weight	10%		5%		15%		25%		45%		100%
	Pts	Score	Pts	Score	Pts	Score	Pts	Score	Pts	Score	
Conference room in office	5	.5	5	.25	5	.75	3	.75	1	.45	2.7
Off-site at local hotel	3	.3	4	.2	4	.6	2	.5	2	.9	2.5
Off-site out of town	1	.1	4	.2	2	.3	1	.25	5	2.25	3.1

The relative weight, or importance, of each factor is a percentage of the total listed underneath each factor. Assign points to each factor to indicate its value using a scale, such as 1 to 5, where 1 is worst and 5 is best. Then, the score for each factor by the location is found by multiplying the weight by its points. Add the scores for each row, and put the results in the Total Points column. For example, the conference room alternative's scores are .5+.25+.75+.75+.45 = 2.7. The alternative with the highest points—an off-site meeting out of town—is the best choice. If you're making a presentation that would benefit from quantitative support, such as the decision-oriented, persuasive, or informational types, be sure to consider including your analysis to add more weight to what you're presenting.

Step 3: Select the Best Alternative

Using a quantitative approach to making a decision can lead to greater confidence in the choice. But you shouldn't ignore the value of qualitative information. In fact, the weighting and ranking table discussed above can help you assign values to this information. These variables often can carry more weight than the computed values in Step 2, and may cause you to choose an alternative with a lower EMV. Some additional questions to ask before finalizing your choice should include:

- What qualitative factors need to be considered, and do they carry enough weight to discount one or more of the options?
- Does this alternative make sense for the long term?
- Can you realistically implement the alternative, given the amount of time and resources you have available?
- Can you live with the choice even if the outcome is not perfect, or if some unconsidered factors arise after you implement it?
- How comfortable are you with the decision?

Step 4: Make an Action Plan

Once the decision is made, you need to figure out the steps for making it happen. By this point, you should have a good idea of what you need the outcome to look like. For your company's retail space decision, it's the small boutique store in full operation with staff and merchandise. Think about how long each step will take, and whether steps can be done at the same time. Line up the resources—people, finances, equipment, and so on. Pick someone to manage the implementation so there's a point person to keep it on budget and on schedule. Decide how you're going to manage any human or behavioral issues— regular communication, training schedules, and ways to transition from old to new.

Set milestones so everyone knows when big pieces are finished and can see progress against the plan. Project management software might be a good choice for a complex project because it can help schedule resources, track budgets, match team member skills to tasks, manage materials and supplies, and calculate critical paths to highlight activities that will hold up progress if they fall behind schedule. The type of presentation most likely to be given during this step is informational because all parties participating in the decision need to know the plan and their duties.

Step 5: Launch and Monitor

You've made your choice and developed your plan. Now you can take action! As events unfold, you can track progress and make mid-course corrections if something doesn't go according to plan. The types of presentations given during this step include informational status updates, instructional training sessions, and perhaps even motivational talks to rally the troops or prop up sagging morale when events don't go smoothly.

Step 6: Check the Results

Good managers check the accuracy of their decisions to see whether they made the right choice. After your company opens the small boutique store, for example, you'll collect data on sales revenue, customer feedback, and economic market conditions. Did everything turn out as expected? If not, what happened, and what corrective action now should be taken? The results of this last step can help you make better decisions the next time. The type of presentations usually given at this point is informational, with an overview of how the process went, the results, and what your team learned and will do differently the next time.

Think about the last time you had to make a big decision. Maybe you decided which college to attend or what car to buy. Revisit your decision using the steps listed here. Did your decision turn out the way you expected? What will you do differently next time?

_____

_____

_____

_____

Avoiding the Most Common Presentation Mistakes

Think back to your elementary school days when it was time for show and tell. What did most children do? They stood up, rambled a bit, produced a visual aid, and sat back down. In college, the cost of poor presentation skills may be a poor grade or muffled snickers from your classmates as you stumble through your material. That's OK—they probably were not much better when it was their turn to present.

However, now that you're preparing for your career, it's critical that you correct your mistakes and work on your technique because the cost of poor presentation skills will escalate dramatically when you start working. Lack of skill can cost you clients, career advancement, and even your job. Most businesspeople (and even your instructor!) can tell you stories of really bad presentations they've seen or perhaps even given, and the consequences the presenter suffered as a result. To help ensure that presenter isn't you, here are some common mistakes and how to avoid them.

Mistake #1: Splitting Up the Presentation

One common mistake made by teams is splitting up the preparation of the presentation. One person takes the introduction, another takes some of the points in the middle, and someone else works on the ending. When it all gets stitched together, more often than not, it comes off as disjointed and disorganized. That's definitely not the best impression to make.

Another twist on this mistake is to let one person prepare the entire presentation and then dole out speaking parts to the other team members to deliver. Although the presentation may be better organized, the team members who didn't participate in its preparation will often end up reading the points off the slides. Audiences can see right through these types of presentations and usually will discount the credibility of the speakers in this situation. Instead, spend time as a team working through the basic planning and outlining steps so all members understand the message. By creating a common outline as a team, each member can then take a portion of the outline to enhance while keeping it consistent with the rest of the presentation's message.

> What happened the last time you split up your team's presentation preparation in this manner?
> _____
> _____
> _____
> _____

Mistake #2: Failing to Dress to Impress

Just as a professional appearance makes a good impression during a job interview, an audience's first impression of a speaker is also based on appearance. Before a single word is spoken, the audience sizes up the way the presenter looks. Does the person look professional and competent? Will he or she be wasting my time with this presentation?

Think about the roles played by actors in your favorite movies. What was your first impression of their characters when you saw them on the screen? Did you form an early impression of them—good or bad—based solely on how they looked? Your audience will do the same for your "performance." If you need to brush up on what to do, refer back to the pointers in Project 1.

> Try an experiment this week. Pay close attention to how you judge the new people you meet. How often did you let their appearance affect your interaction with them? Did your initial impression prove accurate? Why or why not?
> _____
> _____
> _____
> _____

Mistake #3: Ignoring Body Language

When you communicate with others, how you look and act can overshadow what you say and diminish the power of your message. Research done by Dr. Albert Mehrabian of UCLA found that 55% of what we communicate is nonverbal. Our voices convey 38% of our meaning. The remaining 7% of our message comes from the words we speak.

This means that although the outline of your presentation and the text on your slides play a role in message delivery, it's your voice and body language that make or break the delivery. For example, a nervous laugh can distract a listener by shifting focus to this annoying habit. Avoiding eye contact sends the message that you don't want to connect with your audience or that you can't be trusted. Fidgeting or absentmindedly twirling your hair signals nervousness. Slouching connotes laziness, lack of energy, or disinterest. Glancing at your watch tells everyone you'd rather be someplace else.

Even the placement of your hands sends your audience a nonverbal signal. The best position for your hands is comfortably by your side, in a relaxed position. As you talk, it's fine to use hand gestures to help make a point, but be careful about overdoing it. Figure 5-6 summarizes what some common hand gestures convey to an audience.

As you watch others present, pay attention to their body language. What mannerisms did they exhibit that were distracting or annoying?

_____

_____

_____

_____

Figure 5-6 **Speaker hand positions and what they say to an audience**

Hand gestures	Meaning
Hands at sides	Speaker is comfortable and approachable
Open and outstretched hand	To authoritatively dismiss a comment, direct attention to someone or a visual, or make a statement (Example: "Our client isn't interested in that offer.")
Horizontal slicing or flow	Connotes movement or passing of time (Example: "Today is the last day we can offer the discount. Tomorrow, we implement the new pricing plan.")
Hands on hips	Shows defiance or defensiveness, or issuing a challenge (Example: "I don't like the tone of your voice!")
Hands in pockets	Most often conveys over-confidence or nonchalance (Example: "Yeah, I'm the expert and I know it.")
Hands clasped in front or behind	Indicates a passive or inexperienced presenter; can also indicate vulnerability or that the speaker is withholding something from the audience
Hands clasped at chest height	Most common position; variations include fingers touching (think spider legs), hand rubbing, ring-twisting, nervous pen-clicking, which are passive, nervous gestures
Arms crossed on chest	Tells the audience you are not open to discussion or argument
Hands gesturing while speaking	An acceptable means of emphasizing a point (many people "talk" with their hands); should not be overdone
Hands flailing excessively, or hands that are frozen and never move	Usually signals inexperience or nervousness

Mistake #4: Lacking Passion, Energy, or Authority

You did the research. You know the material. You even may be speaking from extensive personal experience. But if your voice is timid or too soft, the audience will assume you don't know what you are talking about and will discount the value of your presentation. If you speak in a monotone, the audience won't sense your passion and knowledge of the material. However, be careful not to overdo it. Speaking too loudly or using a "know-it-all" tone will quickly turn off audience members and make them stop listening altogether.

When an attendee asks a question, be sure to affirm him or her before answering (Example: "That's a great question. What do the rest of you think?" or "Thanks for asking. Here's what my research revealed."). If you relax, smile, and appear confident, your audience will sense your security, triggering a subconscious feeling of ease and comfort with you.

> Think of a recent presentation you heard. How well did the presenter speak? Too soft, too loud, or just right? What did his or her voice convey to you?
>
> _____
> _____
> _____
> _____

Mistake #5: Avoiding Audience Involvement

When you involve your audience members in your presentation, they will pay closer attention to what you have to say. When your school instructors engage the class in discussions, do you remember more of what's said? Do they use audience response "clickers" or interactive polling software to involve you in the material? If you participated in the discussion, chances are strong that you retained even more. The same thing goes for presentations. You might even try out the polling software provided by polleverywhere.com. It's free and easy to set up a poll in minutes that you can include in your presentation. Audience members can respond using their cell phone text messaging services or through a Web site link. The responses show up immediately in your presentation.

Another easy way to get the audience to participate is to start with a question and invite responses. Stop partway through to discuss a particularly important point. An additional benefit of involving your audience is that you can do a quick check to be sure that your presentation is on-point and relevant to attendees by giving them a chance to talk back and discuss.

> Which type of presentation would you rather attend: one in which you had the chance to participate, or one where you simply sat and listened? Why?
>
> _____
> _____
> _____
> _____

Mistake #6: Using Excessive Non-Words and Fillers

Non-words and fillers are often signs of weakness. Non-words consist of ums, ahs, hms, and other such breaks in speech. Fillers are phrases that don't add any value yet add length to sentences. Both can dilute a speaker's message because they are not essential to the meaning of what's being spoken. At best, they can make you sound unprofessional. At worst, they can distract your audience and make your message incomprehensible. Most people use them occasionally, but in most cases they don't serve any good purpose. Here are a few examples:

- I, um, really, uh, don't know if, ah, I can really, you know, actually do this.
- To be honest with you, we actually can't figure out why the product launch actually failed.
- Like I said, the company's sales revenue, was, I mean, below, uh, expectations.
- Well, I guess we kind of missed our sales target.

Listen to yourself as you speak to your friends or coworkers this week. What non-words and fillers do you use frequently? If you can't identify any, ask someone to listen to you and point them out. Then, make an effort to banish them from your speech.

_____

_____

_____

_____

When non-words—such as "um" and "uh"—are used, the impact of what's being said is diminished. They add no value to communication. Sometimes people use filler words to soften the delivery of bad news or avoid sounding too opinionated—as in "I guess we sort of need to lay off Stephanie and her team," as opposed to "We need to lay off Stephanie and her team." Can you see which one sounds more decisive and direct? As an alternative to filler words, a moment of brief silence is perfectly acceptable.

Rewrite the bulleted examples listed above for greater clarity. Do you see the potential for a more meaningful presentation?

_____

_____

_____

_____

Mistake #7: Having Technical Difficulties without a Plan B

Most experienced presenters can tell you about a time when their presentation didn't go exactly as planned. For example, the Internet connection went down, the computer wouldn't display properly on the screen, the projector bulb burned out during the presentation, the room was set up incorrectly, handouts didn't get printed…and the list goes on. Those same presenters also will tell you that although such mishaps can be problematic, having a backup plan saved the presentation and their reputations. Often, just arriving at the presentation location early and testing out the technology, any links to the Internet, and other audio-visual resources in the room will be enough to identify whether there will be issues. At a minimum, consider backing up your presentation on a flash drive or on cloud storage, such as live.com's SkyDrive. By arriving early, you'll have time to take corrective action or enact your Plan B without panicking.

Arriving early also helps you start to build rapport with your audience. By greeting each person as he or she arrives and casually chatting with each one, you'll help to make your audience feel welcome and ease any presentation butterflies you may have.

For your next presentation, think about what could go wrong. What contingency plans should you make now in case those things happen? If you appear to be in control of the situation, how will that reflect on you as an employee and presenter?

_____

_____

_____

_____

Mistake #8: Unnecessarily Distributing Handouts

Many speakers provide printed copies of their presentation slides at the beginning of their speeches. Often, this reduces the need for the audience to take notes on each slide as it's presented. Yet what usually happens is that the audience starts to read through the handouts as soon as they are distributed, getting ahead of the speaker. This means they stop listening. As they turn the pages, the rustle of paper causes a distraction. Pretty soon, the speaker has lost control over the impact of the message.

Instead of handing out materials before the presentation, tell your audience that a summary of your presentation points will be distributed at the end of your session. This way, they can write a few notes only if they feel it's necessary, but they won't skip ahead to the end and miss the great information you deliver. On occasion, you also may want to provide a handout specifically designed to support detailed information you plan to discuss during the presentation. Wait and distribute this handout when you get to that point; otherwise, your audience immediately will start to read it when it's given out, which could throw your presentation off-track.

Think about your next presentation. What types of handouts are needed, if any?

_____

_____

_____

_____

PowerPoint Skills Every Presenter Knows

PowerPoint Dos and Don'ts

If you go to enough meetings at school or work, you'll quickly discover that some people don't like PowerPoint. Yet if you probe a bit deeper, you'll discover that the problem isn't the software; it's the way the presenters use—or more precisely, *abuse*—the tool in the course of delivering their material. So blaming PowerPoint for bad presentations is like trying to blame word processing software for badly written term papers or newspaper articles.

The fact is that PowerPoint, as a presentation software program, is nothing more than a means for organizing a presenter's speech with visual support. A well-organized and planned presentation will be enhanced by the judicious use of PowerPoint's capabilities. But there's no way it can turn a poorly conceived idea into a winning and compelling presentation.

Here is a list of PowerPoint dos and don'ts that you should consider for your future presentations. If the list looks too daunting, remember that following the presentation preparation steps discussed earlier will help you create PowerPoint presentations that are engaging, interesting, and well worth the time your audience will invest in watching and listening to you.

Dos

- **Start with a title slide.**
  Display this slide on the screen before your audience members arrive. This will cue them that they are in the right location. Include the title of your presentation and your name on the slide.

- **Use a consistent theme.**
  A slide show that implements different layouts, color schemes, fonts, or mismatched graphical elements will appear confusing, busy, and distracting to an audience. Instead, select one of the many themes available in PowerPoint that will best suit the purpose of your presentation.

- **Include only simple and relevant pictures, charts, and graphics.**
  The most important part of your presentation is what you say, not the graphics. It's important to underscore your words with visual support, but the graphic elements—whether charts, pictures, or photos—should be easy to read and must relate to what you plan to say.

- **Use audio cues sparingly.**
  The best audio signals are those that draw attention to a significant point you want to make. For example, a speech about increasing profit from a new product introduction could use the sound of a cash register's cha-ching at the peak of the presentation. However, using the sound repeatedly will get old really fast. If you're in doubt about whether the sound effect will enhance what you have to say, consider leaving it out.

- **Use custom animations sparingly.**
  For example, if you have a slide with multiple bullet points, you can use entrance animations to keep the focus on each point as you discuss it. When a slide pops on the screen with all its points revealed, the audience automatically starts to read each one. To do this, they stop listening. So if you want to talk about each point separately, bring them in one at a time as you need them to support what you are saying.

- **Layer complex charts, text, or graphics in small groups.**
  Sometimes there's no getting around a detailed or complex chart to help explain a point. In this case, break the image into small pieces that can be displayed in a layered sequence. Use distinctly different colors to help differentiate the visual elements. This not only helps focus the audience's attention on the part of the image you want to discuss, it also keeps attendees from getting confused as to which section of the image you're referencing when you speak.

- **Use simple fonts in a size large enough to be read from the back of the room.**
  A clean font that's no smaller than size 24 or 28 is usually a good choice for readability. Minimize the mixing of fonts in your presentation so the theme remains clean and consistent.

- **Employ the 7-7 Rule.**
  The 7-7 Rule suggests using no more than seven bullet points per slide, with no more than seven words per bullet. Many presenters use fewer than this number to keep their slides simple and looking clean.

- **Press the *W* or *B* key to temporarily clear the screen.**
  When the W key is pressed during a slide show, it brings up a blank white screen. Pressing it a second time restores the slide show. The B key does the same thing, except the screen changes to a blank black background. Pressing it a second time restores the slide show where you left off.

- **Use dark text on a light background.**
  For maximum contrast and readability, a good presentation will use a dark-colored font on a light or white background to make it easy for the audience to quickly read the content. If nothing else, a simple black font on a white background is a safe way to go.

- **Tell a good story.**
  When a presenter stands up and simply delivers the content listed on each PowerPoint slide, many audience members wonder what value the speaker added by simply talking through the points. After all, the audience can read. Instead, get creative! Tell a good story or anecdote that relates to the points on the slide or to the message being delivered. This will help strengthen the message and boost retention of the main points. Who doesn't like a good story? If you need notes to help you remember your talking points, a few bullets on a notecard—not full sentences or paragraphs!—is fine.

Based upon the presentations you've seen and given, what additional PowerPoint dos need to be added to the list?

_____

_____

_____

_____

Don'ts

Nothing diminishes the credibility of a speaker faster than a poorly designed presentation. No matter how smart or knowledgeable you are, the visual impression you give your attendees will stay with them longer and more strongly than the words you speak (refer back to the section on body language). One sure way to make a bad impression is to violate the list of PowerPoint dos previously listed. In addition, here are a few don'ts that should be considered for your future presentations.

- **Don't skip the titles on each slide.**
  Slide titles give the audience a clue as to the focus of the slide's points. If you leave them off, your audience won't be able to follow the logical flow of your presentation.

- **Don't layer text on top of a busy background graphic.**
  When the background graphic is too bold or busy, it will compete with the text layered on top of it. If you choose to employ a background graphic, tone it down by changing the color boldness or contrast so that it appears faint.

- **Don't rely solely on the automated spelling and grammar check features.**
  One sure way to reduce your credibility as a presenter is to have typographical errors in your presentation. The embedded spell-check and grammar-check features in PowerPoint don't catch everything. Instead, do an old-fashioned, non-automated read-through of your presentation slides. If you are not confident in your spelling or grammar abilities, have someone you trust check your presentation for you.

- **Don't overly animate your slides.**
  Overly animated slides are another way to turn off your audience. With too much action on the screen, the viewer will stop listening in order to watch what's happening on the slide. PowerPoint comes equipped with many different slide entrance/exit, transition, and motion paths, yet the vast majority are simply too busy for a professional presentation. It's fine to use a simple entrance animation, such as Appear, for individual bullet points, but resist the temptation to show off your animation expertise by using the flashier custom animation options. The last thing you want is for your audience to remember the motion show you gave instead of your presentation's point.

- **Don't apply strange combinations of colors, themes, fonts, or styles.**
  Spend some time getting acquainted with all of the color, theme, font, and style choices offered by PowerPoint. Then, use only those that will enhance your message and not overpower or diminish what you have to say. When choosing presentation

colors, avoid deep, saturated blue hues, such as cobalt blue. The reason is that the normal human eye can't properly process the red and blue wavelengths that constitute this color. Instead of crisp and clear contents, they'll appear fuzzy around the edges. If you've ever noticed how blurry blue holiday lights look, you've experienced this effect.

- **Don't use numbered lists with contents that aren't in any special sequence.**
  A numbered list implies a sequential order or series of steps to be followed. If the items in your list do not have to be performed in any particular order, then use bullet points instead of numbers to separate them.

- **Don't display data-intensive charts or graphs.**
  Busy illustrations force the audience to spend time trying to decode what the image is telling them. This means they will stop listening to you while they try to process what's displayed on the screen. If the point of a graphic or chart is to simplify a message to help the viewer understand the point quickly, the last thing you want to do is put so much content into the image that it becomes incomprehensible. You always can distribute a handout with the underlying detail for a graph or chart if the audience needs additional content to understand your point.

- **Don't create too many slides.**
  One common mistake most inexperienced presenters make is creating too many slides to support their presentation. What usually ends up happening is that the presenter runs short on time, so he or she will race through the slides in an effort to finish up. Consequently, important points in the message are skipped, which may end up confusing the audience or lead to a weak and ineffective closing.

- **Don't put too much text on each slide.**
  Almost as bad as having too many slides is putting too much text on the slides you do show. Instead of following the 7-7 Rule, putting entire sentences or paragraphs on a slide compels the audience to stop listening and to read what's on the screen. If you do intend for the audience to read what's written, such as a quote, then either stop talking so they can focus on reading, or read the slide's content verbatim.

Most of the PowerPoint don'ts deal with presentations that are cluttered and overdone. As you prepare your presentations, keep in mind that less is more. With *less* visual distraction, your audience will remember *more* of your message—and that's the whole point!

Based upon the presentations you've seen and given, what additional PowerPoint don'ts should be added to the list?

_____

_____

_____

_____

Technology Skills—Adding Speaker Notes in PowerPoint Slide Shows and Preparing Handouts

As you've learned, effective presentations take time to prepare. Organizing and creating the actual presentation in PowerPoint is just one part, however. Most speakers like to keep track of notes or comments that accompany each slide so they can remember them during their presentations. These notes can be added to slides in a presentation, which then can be printed to replace the need for separate note cards when giving a presentation. You also can print different views of your presentation to use as handouts for your attendees so they can take notes and remember your key points afterward.

The Technology Skills steps cover these skills:

• Add speaker notes to a PowerPoint presentation.
• View and print speaker notes.
• Print audience handouts.

To add speaker notes to a PowerPoint presentation:

Speaker notes are useful for helping a speaker recall the main points on each slide in a presentation. In PowerPoint, they appear in the Notes pane below the Slide pane in Normal view. See Figure 5-7.

Figure 5-7   **Location of the Notes pane in PowerPoint's Normal view**

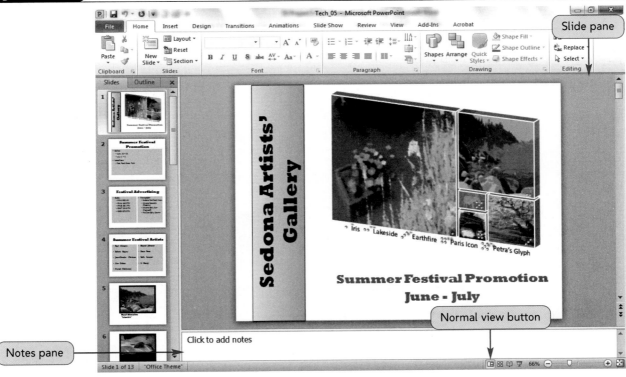

Speaker notes don't appear anywhere on the slide during a slide show. To add notes to any presentation, follow these steps:

TIP

Enter speaker notes in numbered or bulleted form instead of full sentences and paragraphs to make them easier to read when printed.

1. Open the file **Tech_05.pptx** located in the Project.05 folder included with your Data Files, and then, to avoid altering the original file, save the document as **(YourName)_ArtPromo.pptx** on your local drive or other storage location.

2. If it's not already selected, go to Slide 1 in the presentation. Be sure Normal view is selected.

3. Click in the **Notes** pane for Slide 1, and then type **Hand out information packets**.

4. Go to Slide 2 in the presentation. Click in the **Notes** pane, and then type **Describe the logistics for visitors to Red Rock State Park**.

5. Go to Slide 5 in the presentation. Click in the **Notes** pane, and then type the following:

- **Raul Almeira native of Seville, Spain**
- **Makes his home in Lake Tahoe, California**
- **Featured artist at the festival for the past three years**

6. Click in the **Notes** pane for Slides 6 through 13, and then add notes for each artist that are similar to the note for Slide 5. You can make up this information since this is just for practice.

7. Save your presentation.

To view and print speaker notes in a PowerPoint presentation:

1. With your presentation open, go to Slide 1.

2. Click the **View** tab on the PowerPoint Ribbon.

3. In the Presentation Views group, click the **Notes Pages** button. The speaker note that you added appears directly below the slide thumbnail on the page. One slide per page appears in this view. See Figure 5-8.

| Figure 5-8 | Notes Page view |

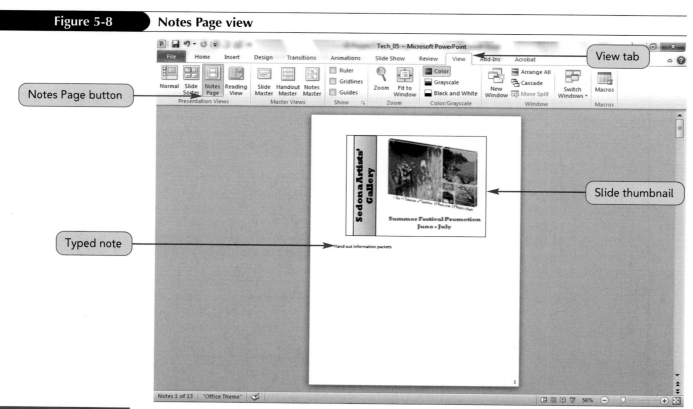

4. To print speaker notes, click **File>Print**. If necessary, click the **Printer** button to select the correct printer.

5. Under Settings, click the **Full Page Slides** down arrow button. This is the default print option. From the drop-down box, select **Notes Pages**. See Figure 5-9.

| Figure 5-9 | Printing Notes Pages with speaker notes |

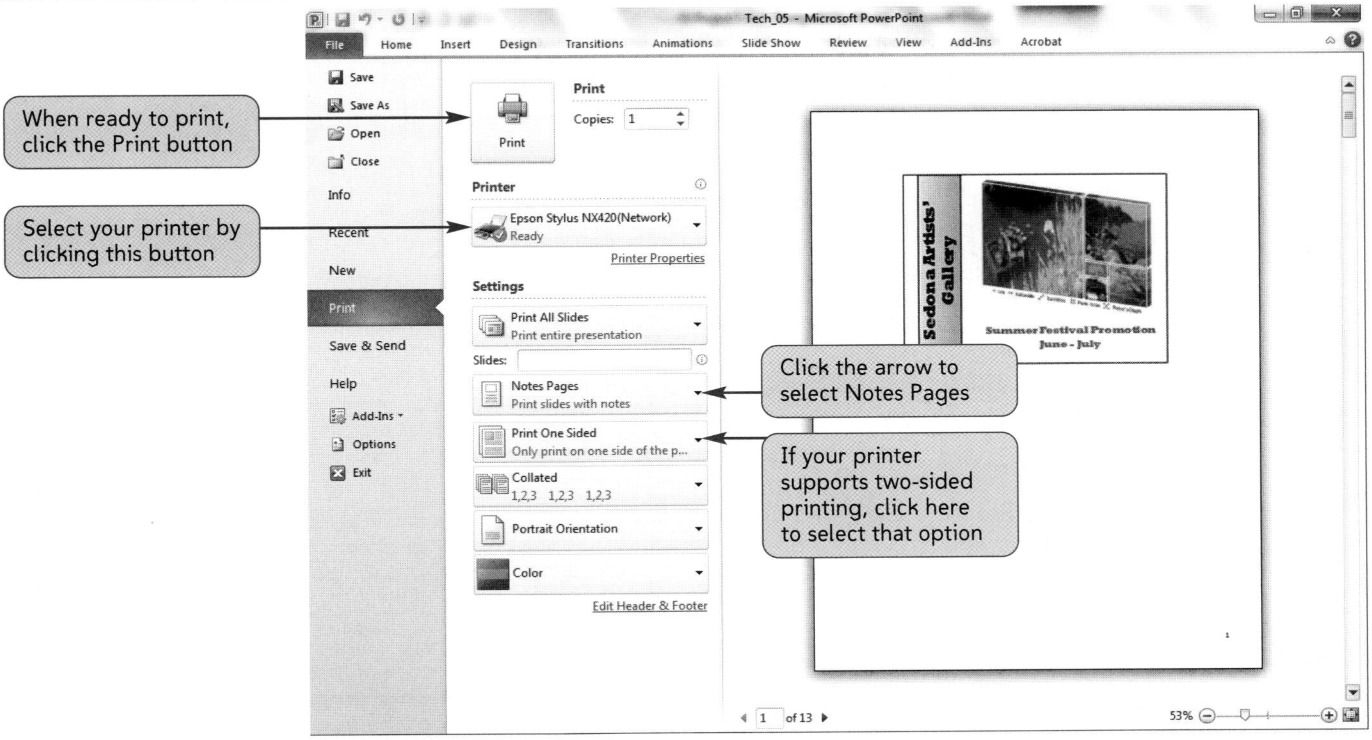

When ready to print, click the Print button

Select your printer by clicking this button

Click the arrow to select Notes Pages

If your printer supports two-sided printing, click here to select that option

▶ **6.** Click **Print**.

To print audience handouts:

▶ **1.** With your presentation open, click **File>Print**.

▶ **2.** Under Settings, click the **Full Page Slides** down arrow button. From the drop-down box, select the Handouts option that best suits your needs. To print hand-outs with space for notes to the right of each slide, click **3 Slides**. See Figure 5-10.

▶ **3.** Click **Print**.

Figure 5-10 **Printing audience handouts**

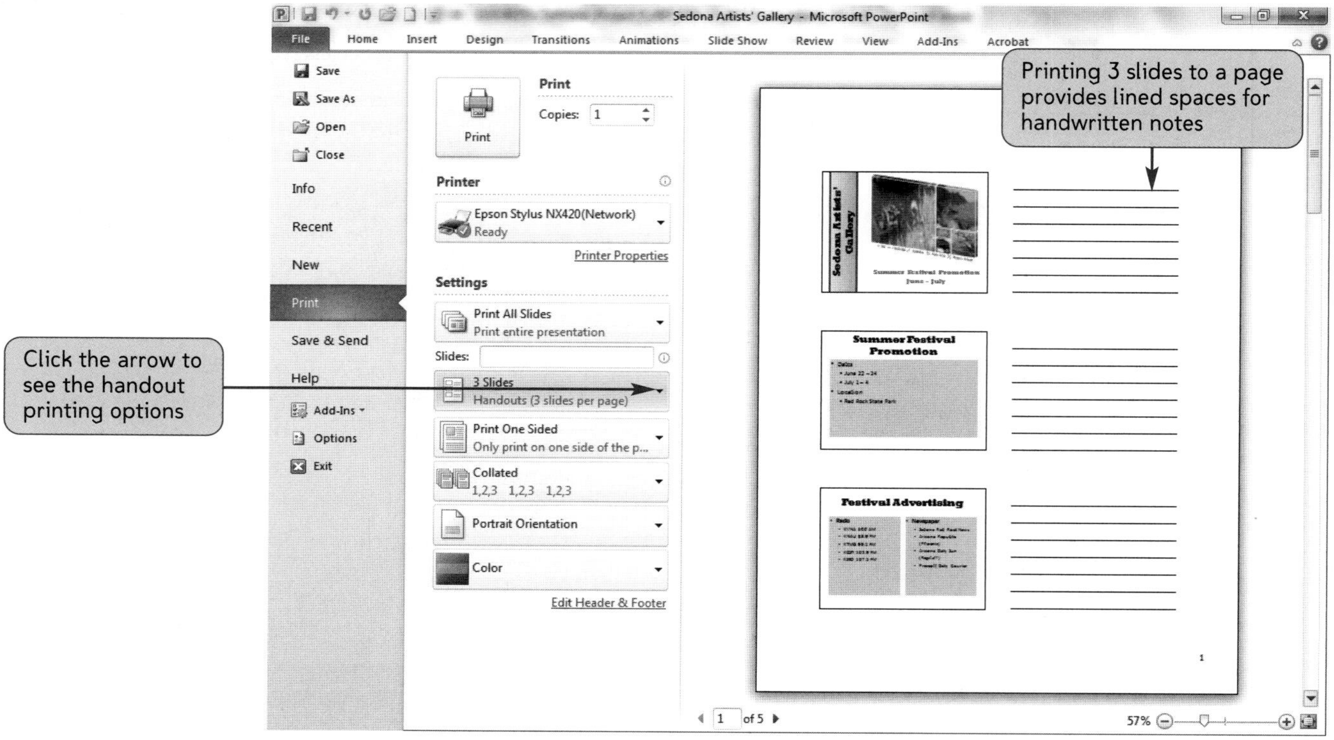

PRACTICE

Emerging Technologies Presentation

There's never a dull moment in the world of technology. This assignment gives you the opportunity to create your own PowerPoint presentation on an emerging technology.

1. Choose one of the emerging technologies or trends from the following list or find one on your own (ask your instructor for permission first):
   - Web 2.0 and Web 3.0 (Define the terms first, and then explore Wikis, blogs, Twitter, YouTube, and other resources.)
   - Social networks (Go beyond Facebook and LinkedIn.)
   - Web collaboration and content portability (*Hint*: Examine what Google is doing; explore SkyDrive, MobileMe, cloud computing.)
   - Mobile broadband and telecommunications technologies (Consider what's happening with new devices, such as smartphones, e-readers, and tablets such as the iPad.)
   - Crowdsourcing (Wikipedia is just one example.)
2. Research the topic.
3. Create an informational PowerPoint presentation. In your presentation, provide an overview of the technology or trend, the effect on people, business or society, the global implications, and why it's an important trend for society, education, or the workplace. Provide examples and use media to support your presentation.

REVISE

Turning a Good Presentation into a Great One

Jill and Marcus created an informational presentation for their team in this project's video episode. After watching it, you think there's room for improvement.

1. Open the PowerPoint start file, **Revise_05.pptx**.
2. Modify Jill and Marcus' presentation to fit your ideas of what an informational presentation should look like.
3. Add speaker notes to each slide.
4. Save your presentation as **(YourName)_EncoreStatus.pptx**.
5. Print your presentation's speaker notes.

CREATE

Project 4 Report Presentation: Sell Your Team's Location to the Encore Staff

Catherine Parker has read through the proposal that your team created in Project 4 for the location of the company's next annual meeting. In the event your team's location proposal is chosen over those submitted by other Encore teams, she'd like your team to prepare a PowerPoint presentation that she could use to unveil the winning location to the entire staff at the next quarterly training meeting. Using what you've learned about PowerPoint and presentations in this project, create a persuasive presentation that's sure to generate excitement among the consultants as they anticipate a few working days away from the office with their colleagues.

1. Meet with your Project 4 team to plan your presentation.
2. Open PowerPoint 2010.
3. Create your presentation, complete with text, graphics, and animations.
4. Add speaker notes to each slide.

5. Save your presentation as **(TeamName)_Encore.pptx**.

6. Print your speaker notes and print audience handouts (three slides to a page).

Case Study 1

Encore Consulting: The Big Presentation Watch the final Encore video episode to see what happened at the meeting with Catherine Parker. If required by your instructor, fill in the **VideoCritique_Worksheet_05.docx** with your answers; save your file, and then print it to submit to your instructor. Answer these questions:

1. Evaluate the PowerPoint presentation prepared by Jill and Marcus. What did they do well? What could they improve for next time?

_____

_____

_____

_____

2. Evaluate Jill and Marcus' business attire. Does it seem appropriate for an internal meeting (i.e., no clients present)? How does their attire compare to that of the other consultants and Catherine Parker?

_____

_____

_____

_____

3. How well did Jill and Marcus deliver their presentation? What suggestions for improvement would you offer them? Be sure to consider their PowerPoint slide show, their individual presentation skills, and the printed materials they used.

_____

_____

_____

_____

4. What do you think about the behavior of the other meeting participants?

_____

_____

_____

_____

5. Assume you are a new consultant assigned to Jill and Marcus' team. As the newest team member, you are given the responsibility of preparing the team's project update presentation. Using the material in this project and the video episode featuring Jill and Marcus, what will you do differently, and why?

_____

_____

_____

_____

Case Study 2

APPLY

Using a Decision Table: What Should Encore Do? As Encore's consulting practice has grown, so has its staff. Although most staff members are on assignment at various client locations throughout the year, the office space Catherine Parker leased when she started the organization can no longer handle the client meetings and staff activity on a daily basis. Catherine recently engaged the services of a commercial real estate specialist who has come up with two different locations for Encore to consider:

- The first location is a downtown high-rise building, with enough space for the existing staff plus room for an additional 50% growth. Catherine expects that moving to this space will result in a net income of $550,000 in a favorable economy, and a net loss of $200,000 in an unfavorable economy.

- The second location is a suburban office park housing a new, single-level contemporary building with plenty of free parking. Catherine's estimate of net income is $400,000 in a favorable economy, and the estimated net loss is $40,000 in an unfavorable economy.

1. Using the technique explained for decision making under risk, calculate the EMV of each location, assuming the probability of a favorable economy is 60% and the probability of an unfavorable economy is 40%.

> Write your calculations here. Which is the best choice?
>
> _____
> _____
> _____
> _____

2. Assume that no probabilities can be assigned for the economic outlook. Using the technique described for decision making under uncertainty, determine which location is the best choice.

> Is it different from the result obtained using the EMV calculations?
>
> _____
> _____
> _____
> _____

3. After you have completed both sets of calculations, prepare a short informational presentation to explain the decision.

APPLY

Case Study 3

Using a Weighting and Ranking Table: Office Furniture Replacement Decision Assume you're the office manager for a regional medical center. You've been asked to replace the aging lobby furniture for your outpatient clinic. After doing some research and contacting local interior designers, you've come up with several possible choices. The styles you're interested in are:

- Techno Modern, as shown in Figure 5-11
- Rustic Comfort, as shown in 5-12
- Minimalist, as shown in Figure 5-13
- Upscale Trendy, as shown in Figure 5-14

| Figures 5-11 | Example of Techno Modern lobby furniture |

Alexey Kashin/Shutterstock.com

| **Figures 5-12** | **Example of Rustic Comfort lobby furniture** |

hagit berkovich/Shutterstock.com

| **Figures 5-13** | **Example of Minimalist lobby furniture** |

Alexey Kashin/Shutterstock.com

Figures 5-14 **Example of Upscale Trendy lobby furniture**

Gina Smith/Shutterstock.com